T012956B

In the Spirit of Jesus

Miriam Therese Winter

authorHOUSE®

AuthorHouse™
1663 Liberty Drive
Bloomington, IN 47403
www.authorhouse.com
Phone: 833-262-8899

Published by AuthorHouse 08/28/2020

ISBN: 978-1-7283-6997-6 (sc)
ISBN: 978-1-7283-6995-2 (hc)
ISBN: 978-1-7283-6996-9 (e)

Library of Congress Control Number: 2020915034

Print information available on the last page.

I did not intend to write another book.
My cosmic clock is ticking.
There are multiple things to attend to
as the sun begins its steady descent
on the landscape of my life.
However, as always, ubiquitous Spirit has other plans
and knows just how to entice me
to dare to do what needs to be done,
no matter what the cost.
Once again, I feel commissioned
to share a new way of seeing the sacred
in these unpredictable times.
This is a book about Jesus:
a living, loving, inclusive Jesus.
I am convinced the spirit of Jesus,
source of my inspiration,
is with me, urging me on.

Miriam Therese Winter

Spirit sings songs of love
everlastingly,
all that lives an echo of
Love's diversity.

Love is easy when we feel
filled with words of praise;
yet sometimes our prayers conceal
less than loving ways.

Love can transform all we do,
teach us how to be
loving to each other through
all adversity.

Love our God with all your heart
in the ones you see,
every day a brand new start.
Love wholeheartedly.

It is amazing how a new perspective
spills over into everything.

CONTENTS

With grateful thanks to my community of
Medical Mission Sisters & Associates in North America
and in healing ministries around the world,
and to Eunice Cudzewicz, MMS, for the All One graphic;
to President Joel Lohr, Dr. Yehezkel Landau,
and my colleagues and friends
at Hartford Seminary, my academic home;
and to all who have shared Spirit with me
in classes, conversations, celebrations, and song.

INTRODUCTION

What can I say about Jesus that would add new insight to a Christian's understanding of the man from Galilee? Scriptures, manuscripts, creeds, sermons, prayers, rites, rituals, and centuries of sung praise fill our ancient archives and ubiquitous sanctuaries. Of even more significance, Jesus, who is so much larger than life, dwells in the depths of the faith-filled heart and continues to be, for many, source of everlasting life. Son of God? Superstar? Does anyone know who you really are?

Ironically, the one we call upon to be a harbinger of peace, and an example of justice and mercy, is often the reason why people today continue to divide and exclude. Instead of seeing Jesus as a unifying force for all Christians everywhere, socio-political bigotry and systemic bias expressed in multi-faceted ways in the name of Jesus stifle the transformative power inherent within our faith traditions. We have rejected, condemned, killed one another based on our interpretations of the one we call Prince of Peace.

We need a new narrative. We need to acknowledge there is more to the story of Jesus of Nazareth, his life and his mission, than what we profess and proclaim. This missing dimension – a critical component – is especially relevant now, not only for historical accuracy, but also for helping us reimagine ways of honoring the inherent integrity of all God's creation. With the closing of churches and the growing dissolution of clergy and community, ecclesial models may not be the framework we will be handing on. Without a more inclusive and compassionate understanding of the one we know as Jesus, not only churches, but our beloved planet, with all of its inhabitants and nature's graced diversity, cannot – will not – survive.

This book about Jesus focuses on decisive turning points in the life of one driven by a cosmic vision. Sources reveal an individual filled with prophetic energy, or in contemporary terms, quantum potentiality. From a twentieth-first century perspective, his spirit was open to those cosmic forces that gave birth to our universe, to energies encompassing countless galaxies in deep space and beyond. In a sense, his spirit was larger than life, reflecting a capacity to move beyond the imposed limitations of our humanity. That same energy was present within ancient mystics and sages from the very beginning of civilization and resonates in us here and now. This is the touchstone of evolution. In the physical and in the spiritual realms, we are forever becoming.

Today there is an urgency to think and act differently. We humans need to change how we relate to diversity. That is the only way this precious planet will continue to be home for humanity. Here is a way to begin.

Embrace a transformed understanding of what it means to be Christian. Cultivate a climate of reconciliation among denominations and within congregations, allowing diversity in all its forms to be present and to flourish.

Seek forgiveness from Jewish communities for centuries of misunderstanding and hurtful behaviors that are a shameful part of our past. Resolve to turn a page, and in the spirit of Jesus, make efforts to begin again.

Make restitution for slavery. Support efforts for systemic change encapsulated in the mantra, "Black Lives Matter."

Acknowledge the injustices perpetrated among Native Americans. Embrace the wisdom of indigenous peoples that many are hungering for.

Celebrate gay and lesbian couples and the LGBTQ community. Treat all as members of one diverse and evolving human family.

Welcome Muslims, Hindus, Sikhs and all God's grace-full people into a global society located all around the world.

What would Jesus do with such a systemic change in attitude during these turbulent times? Reflect on that, alone and with others. Prepare to be surprised.

More than ever, we need examples of how to live faith fully in a world that has outgrown its borders, revealing the remains of quantum footprints virtually everywhere.

Quantum energy is ubiquitous and instantaneous, propelling explorations in space, constantly giving rise to inventive impulses closer to home. In the invisible realm, quantum reality is both this and that simultaneously, linking energies within us to the world around us. Future generations will take this for granted, while many among us here and now will never understand the science of quantum reality, even though we exist within it. From a faith perspective, energy is Spirit at the heart of all creation, not a separate reality in a Trinitarian entity set apart from us all.

Finally, consider this. How will Jesus fit within a framework of faith for future generations? We have stifled the transformative potential of the son of Mary, ignored his Jewish identity, and missed the point of his prophetic passion. Jesus was a human being who, in his time and on his terms, was simply being human, thereby witnessing to all the graced potential in our species. At times it seems he was pushed beyond the limits of human endurance, but aren't we all?

Jesus has been for me, and can be for many, a tangible manifestation of a grace-full humanity, an example of how we humans can continue to be a beneficial link in the evolutionary chain.

Human Being
you and me
sparks of cosmic energy:
being human
let us be
manifestation
celebration
of our sacred destiny
channeling divinity
deep within humanity.
Hearts open wide.
Grace personified.

Part One

TRANSFORMATIVE PRESENCE
• COMING OF AGE •

Time
the timeless eternal:
that which we bring to birth
brings us back
to our beginnings
and helps us
begin
again.

CHAPTER ONE

IN THE BEGINNING

Sometimes, when things seem utterly confusing, when we feel like our world is spinning out of control, it is wise to pause for a while and go back to the beginning. Reflect on what it was that we needed to fix or reimagine, and then begin again. This is especially so when the subject at hand happens to be our in-the-beginning God.

Absolute certitude had fortified our belief that our planet was the center of the universe and that nothing else was out there. Until now. In the wake of astrophysics and aerospace discoveries, this assertion is no longer viable. The same is true for many of the deeply rooted convictions regarding our faith traditions. Some of these still have value. Far too many do not.

The universe today is no longer just our village, our town, our city, our country, or even our continent. So much of what we have considered absolute – individually or collectively – we now perceive as relative because of the astonishing quantum leaps that have occurred in recent times. It is no longer possible to go forward without a consideration of how what we do and what we demand will affect the rest of the world. We now know so much more, via the internet, about who and what is out there. The surge of electronic interconnectivity has been astonishing, and there is no end in sight. This graced evolutionary outcome has already moved to another level when it comes to faith and belief.

As our global associations continue to expand, what will it take to achieve solidarity and a genuine concern for the many others different from ourselves? Religion has helped in a variety ways, but it has also contributed to mass destruction and the global mess we have made. Individual and group connections, however, have been taking quantum leaps, moving exponentially from one to one and electronically to many, linking people of faith to others nearby or far away. Many are finding common ground with those who differ in significant ways. A new world is emerging. It is the world of Spirit, where we sense what we cannot see.

The challenge that lies ahead for us begins right here at home. In the midst of this seismic shift in intercultural relationships, some of us are committed to resurrecting the spirit of Jesus and redefining our deepest values more inclusively. Who would Jesus be today? How would he behave here and now? Surely, he would encourage us to reach out and bring together, make restitution for systemic wrong, empower those who have been excluded, really be "one nation, under God, with liberty and justice for all." For the first time in human history, we live in an age when those at a distance are just a click away. Our collective cosmic consciousness, from the beginning until now, has been longing for a time such as this. In order to continue moving forward in matters of faith and believing, we need to go back to the beginning before we begin again.

BACKSTORY

In the beginning, there was no beginning, so scientists surmise. Beyond the world we know and love, there are approximately two trillion galaxies, each consisting of billions of stars. This is hard for us to imagine, yet scientific facts stand firm. Our planet, Earth, is located within a spiral galaxy called the Milky Way, which may contain 400 billion stars plus 100 billion planets. In our own observable universe, it is said, there may be 200 billion to two trillion galaxies, a twinkling carpet of dancing lights on certain nights of the year. Earth itself is approximately 4.6 billion years old, and it is within this context that we place the story of Jesus. The opening lines of the Bible, quite simply and succinctly, create a cosmic context for all that is to evolve. This book on the life and meaning of Jesus is hoping to do the same.

> *"In the beginning*
> *God created the heavens and Earth.*
> *Now Earth was a formless void.*
> *There was darkness over the deep.*
> *God's spirit hovered over the water."*
> (Genesis 1:1)
> *God said: "Let us make humanity*
> *in our own image,*
> *in the likeness of ourselves …*
> *God created humanity in the image of Godself,*
> *created them in the image of God,*
> *created them male and female."*
> (Genesis 1:27)

Two key elements of sacred Scripture permeate the rest of this chapter, or more accurately, this book. The first: "God's spirit hovered …." The second: "God created humanity in the image of God, created them male and female." The forming and transforming ethos of Spirit in the opening lines of Genesis is at the heart of this contemporary effort to resurrect the spirit of Jesus. The goal: to reflect more universally on what Jesus was about and what mattered most to him. In this context, there is a second designation for Spirit. Energy. More specifically, Cosmic or Quantum Energy. The metaphor, Divine Energy, is another way of saying "God."

ANOTHER PERSPECTIVE
THE TRANSFORMATIVE SECRET

The story of Jesus began long before the beginning so familiar to us within our Christian tradition. There is more to the nativity narrative than what we celebrate. One of the missing pieces relates to the circumstances of his conception. The popular account from the Gospel of Luke, where a virgin gives birth to a baby boy, shepherds dance, and angels sing is heartwarming and inspiring. During turbulent times, this is precisely what we need to make it through the day. Children reenact the Nativity in their annual Christmas pageants. Shepherds, sages, and sheep look on as a radiant babe on a bed of straw smiles to their sung "Noel." The Gospel according to Matthew, however, hints at a different story. It is not a feel-good one. In fact, it is quite disturbing; and we continue to suppress the shocking evidence it conceals.

Scholars have uncovered a hidden narrative in the ancestry of Jesus. It appears in the genealogy of Joseph recorded in Matthew's gospel at the beginning of chapter one. In the lengthy list of patriarchs that spans fifteen centuries are the names of four women: Tamar, mother of Perez and Zerah; Rahab, mother of Boaz; Ruth, mother of Obed; and the wife of Uriah, who would become the mother of Solomon. Their presence hints at a different story regarding Mary's pregnancy. Matthew's chronicle ends with this declaration: "...and Jacob was the father of Joseph the husband of Mary; of her was born Jesus who is called Christ." Joseph was Mary's husband, but he was not the father of Jesus. This we have always known. Both Gospels make that clear. Luke attributed the origin of Jesus to a miraculous intervention of the Holy Spirit and a virgin giving birth. Subsequently, tradition canonized Mary's perpetual virginity. Matthew conceals the real story behind several tantalizing clues. He names four women in his genealogy. All four women were prostitutes or victims of rape. Historically, they play a significant role in the evolution of Israel, and tradition honors them as instruments of the Divine.

What if this understanding of Mary's pregnancy had shaped our Christian faith perspective? What would it have meant for women to know that Mary, the mother of Jesus, may have had to declare "me too"? Would angels still sing "Glory to God" or would angels weep?

What effect would that have had regarding religious roles and gender sanctions and criteria for the priesthood? Most important of all: what would that alternate story have meant with regard to our relationship with Jesus? No doubt, things would have been vastly different if Luke had recorded the following, which also states that the child within Mary's womb is of the Holy Spirit. All mothers-to-be, including those who were violated, would find themselves within it.

> *"Mary, a Jewish maiden, lived in the town of Nazareth in southern Galilee. She would soon marry a man named Joseph. They agreed she would remain a virgin until they were husband and wife. One day something unimaginable occurred. When Mary realized she was with child, she was greatly distressed. Then she heard a voice within her say: "Mary, do not be afraid. You have found favor with God. You will bear a son; and you shall name him Jesus. The Spirit of God will accompany you and the Divine will overshadow you. The child to be born is holy and is indeed a child of God."*

The text aligns with tradition. The words of the Spirit to Mary remain. This baby is a child of the Spirit. This baby is a child of God. Ask yourself: "Isn't every child?" We need to embrace this perspective now - universally.

Geographically, Nazareth was a small town nestled within the foothills of lower Galilee. It was located approximately 64 miles north of Jerusalem. Encircled by nature's pristine beauty and tucked into a valley, this was home for both Mary and Joseph. Because the country was under Roman occupation, it was likely that a military outpost could have existed nearby. Imagine this for a moment. Young men assigned to duty out there in the middle of nowhere. A maiden goes out for an evening stroll. Isolation. Temptation. Violation? We will never know. What a wellspring of healing and spiritual support would be available to so many women should we accept the possibility of a different set of circumstances regarding the conception of Jesus. God in the midst of life as it is. That is incarnation.

A remarkable coincidence pushes the narrative in a different direction. Mary's relative, Elizabeth, convinced she was past her childbearing years, announces she too is pregnant. Two childless women. Both expecting a baby under inexplicable circumstances. One with her life ahead of her, the other getting on in years. Both miraculously conceive, or so the story goes. In one sense, it was another miracle. Had Elizabeth really been sterile, or was Zechariah impotent? Did the news of Mary's pregnancy suddenly rearrange that narrative? Mary goes to be with her elder, as village women do; and when their storylines intersect, we sense a deep connection in their canticle of praise. The specifics of that memorable moment are the stuff of metaphor. The extraordinary gift of life within both is set in a cosmic context. Their words of comfort and encouragement are a mantra to women everywhere in circumstances such as theirs.

While still a doctoral candidate at Princeton Theological Seminary in 1978, using words attributed to Mary, I wove this quantum moment into a hymn of praise.

> My soul gives glory to my God.
> My heart pours out its praise.
> God lifted up my lowliness
> in many marvelous ways.
>
> My God has done great things for me:
> yes, holy is God's name.
> All people will declare me blessed,
> and blessings they shall claim.
>
> From age to age, to all who fear,
> such mercy love imparts,
> dispensing justice far and near,
> dismissing selfish hearts.
>
> Love casts the mighty from their thrones,
> promotes the insecure,
> leaves hungry spirits satisfied,
> the rich seem suddenly poor.

Praise God whose loving covenant
supports those in distress,
remembering past promises
with present faithfulness.

Even though the details are forever lost, we know something meaningful happened. The impossible became possibility. Many times women have said about life, "It's a miracle!" A child in the womb? A miracle! The quantum experience of Mary and Elizabeth lives on through the ages, showing how all such moments transcend the limits of time and situational circumstance. Some experiences are definitive. Others uplift and inspire. Incarnation. Visitation. Decisive turning points for those with hearts open wide enough to let the Spirit in. Metaphor is more powerful than fact. Speaking of facts, the conclusion here is one we ought to question.

> "Mary remained with Elizabeth for about three months and then returned home. When it was time for Elizabeth to deliver her child, she gave birth to a son." (Lk 1:56-58)

Really? Mary stayed all that time, and then left before the main event? Village women – relatives, friends – support a woman about to give birth. They are eager to see the baby. Ordinarily, until after the delivery, nobody goes home. Christianity has done a lot of editing to the story of Jesus. Sometimes it is impossible to separate fact from fiction.

RESURRECTING THE SPIRIT OF JESUS

"In the beginning was the Word:
the Word was with God and the word was God."
(John 1:1)

In the metaphor of "Word," John the Evangelist melds the humanity of Jesus with the stream of quantum energy at the core of all that is.

7

John's mystical revelation heralds Jesus as Divine Messenger of what is seen and yet unseen. Jesus is messenger – there have been many through the ages. He proclaims that Spirit – a Quantum Spirit – is the divine evolutionary force at the heart of all creation, in everyone and everywhere. What would the world we live in be like if this were the defining principle of our global humanity? What if people of faith concurred that Compassion is just another name for the largesse of God.

Some takeaways from those cryptic clues tucked into the infancy narratives shine light on our darkest moments. Be it hope, a plan, a dream, a vision overrun by devastation, grace is never defeated. Spirit is never bound. Seeds sprout. Grass grows. Orchards yield their harvest. With faith in the gift of starting over, we can resurrect what seems to be lost. We can begin again.

> Sing worn and weary Earth.
> Bring the yet unborn to birth.
> All that is buried deep within
> embrace, and let what is new begin.
> Time will tell a different story.
> All will be well. Rejoice! Sing glory!

~ ~ ~

QUANTUM SPARKS / QUANTUM SPIRIT
Personal Reflection on the Reading
What did you find most disturbing, and why?
What did you find most liberating and inspiring, and why?
What points are "keepers" for you?

•

Group Discussion
Gather with others to discuss how you feel about what you read.
Encourage all to share their response to the questions raised above.

•

What are potential outcomes – positive and negative – of this
new perspective regarding Jesus and his mother Mary?

•

How will you be a healing presence in our world here and now?
Share ways to resurrect the spirit of Jesus here and now.

Closing Prayer
"All the World"

ALL THE WORLD

All the world awakens with the rising sun,
morning after morning, blessing everyone.
What have we accomplished when the day is done?
What on Earth is worth our handing on?

Energies that warm us from a distant star
constantly transform us, make us who we are.
Consciousness is cosmic, prone to peace or war.
What will Earth become when we are gone?

Love is everlasting. Love for everyone
spills into the future, shapes what we've begun.
Love's inherent wisdom, with us on the run,
gives us hope to build a world upon.

Words and Music: Miriam Therese Winter
© Medical Mission Sisters 2020

CHAPTER TWO

UPROOTED

"In those days Caesar Augustus issued a decree for a census to be taken. All had to be enrolled, each in his own city. Joseph set out from the town of Nazareth in Galilee and traveled to Judea, to Bethlehem, the city of David, because he was of the house and lineage of David. He went with Mary, his betrothed, who was with child. While they were there, she delivered her firstborn son, wrapped him in swaddling clothes, and laid him in a manger, because there was no place for them in the inn." (Luke 2:1-7)

On her return to Nazareth, after spending three months with Elizabeth, a very pregnant Mary was on the move again. Rome had mandated a census in the territories under its jurisdiction. Everyone had to register. Because Joseph, like so many others, had to return to where he was born, he set out with Mary for Bethlehem, heading south to Judea. The distance: about 90 miles. There may have been just the two of them, or a caravan of travelers, if only for security's sake. They passed through desert and rugged terrain, as well as verdant valleys. Everywhere there were olive groves that offered a moment of respite to folk along the way. The last bit of their journey took them over the hills around Jerusalem and down into Bethlehem.

They would have encountered a groundswell of people who had come, not only to register, but also because the administrative center for the population south of Jerusalem was located nearby. As a result, there really was no available housing anywhere. Literally, there were no rooms in the Inn. However, one could set up a makeshift camp outside in its spacious courtyard. Shade trees, a well with water, and an open area surrounded by a wall allowed weary travelers to unharness and feed their animals, while taking a break for themselves. Most likely, this is where Mary and Joseph settled in for the night, where Mary gave birth to Jesus, and breast-fed her newborn child. Eight days later, they went up to Jerusalem for the circumcision of Mary's baby. Then, without warning, a startling occurrence interrupts this sequence of events, precipitating a turning point that would redefine their lives.

> "An angel appeared to Joseph in a dream and said:
> 'Get up! Take the child and his mother and escape into
> Egypt. Stay there until I tell you it is safe to return. King
> Herod is searching for the boy and he is plotting to kill
> him.' Joseph arose, took the child and his mother, and
> left that night for Egypt, where they remained until
> Herod died." (Mt 2:13-15)

BACKSTORY

What do we really know about the circumstances surrounding the birth of Jesus? Gospel sources differ or they say nothing at all. Even with speculation supported by solid scholarship, there is no definitive conclusion. Facts are enshrouded in mythical meaning and the mystery lingers on. Liturgical traditions dominate and now have a life of their own. Three Kings – the traditional designation – their gifts of gold, incense, and myrrh continue to be an integral part of our Christmas celebrations. With regard to this particular incident within our received tradition, this is what we know.

Soon after Mary had given birth to her child, three sages arrived in Jerusalem. Some say these respected savants from afar were from Arabia. They were seeking a newborn baby boy. The child was divinely favored, they said. There had been an astrological sign. A new star appeared in the heavens and it led them to this place. They wanted to pay him homage before returning home. When word of this reached Herod, he told his aides to find the boy before the Magi did, and ordered them to kill him. It was crucial to eliminate this potential threat to his autocracy.

That decision precipitated a chain of events that radically reoriented the life of the family from Nazareth. They returned home inconspicuously; put their affairs in order; bid farewell to family and friends; and then, under cover of darkness, set out to begin again. After crossing the border into Egypt, they changed location often in order to avoid detection from Herod's ubiquitous spies. Eventually, they would return to Nazareth; but not before Herod had died. By then, Jesus was a little boy, walking or running beside them. His exact age is uncertain – three, perhaps, or four. Old enough to be aware of the universe around him. Finally coming home.

ANOTHER PERPECTIVE

Take a moment to imagine this, all you who are mothers and fathers. Step into someone else's shoes, woolen socks, or sandals. The world is teeming with makeshift camps and temporary shelters, filled to overflowing with families like yours and mine. Here in the USA are masses huddled along our borders. Crammed into flimsy shelters and herded together like sheep, but without a compassionate shepherd, are individual human beings created in the image God. Imagine how you would feel if something similar happened to you or to your family. So many people today are on the verge of destitution. Security is no longer a given, unless it is given to those with nothing by those who have more than enough. What if we saw all displaced people as mirror images of Jesus, and in some ways, a lot like us. All of them seeking safety and a future they can build on. That would call for a different narrative about our collective humanity. So let us consider this.

The vast majority of individuals who are now living in the USA are the result of seeds sown far and wide. Our ancestors came from everywhere over an expanse of time. Willingly or unwillingly, they pulled up roots, settled down, and began all over again. Except for indigenous peoples, the original settlers on this land, we all arrived from somewhere else and our heritage is from elsewhere. Yet quantum Spirit, dwelling in all, can lift us out of our prejudices, our bigotry, and our insular separations by helping us to imagine a new form of ancestry. Our collective heritage is planet Earth. We human beings – all of us – everyone, without exception – are the result of a quantum leap within the Divine milieu. Gaia is a precious gem enhancing Love's firmament, her multifaceted offspring reflecting divine creativity.

RESURRECTING THE SPIRIT OF JESUS

The liturgical celebration of Epiphany features Three Kings from the Orient seeking a newborn baby, a stranger to them all. The gifts they bring, tradition says, are gold, incense, and myrrh. The feast is a cultural favorite, and it is deeply symbolic. Epiphany means manifestation, or enlightenment. At the very beginning of the life of Jesus, foreigners – strangers – driven by an impulse they could not define, traversed established boundaries to follow the path of a star. Some of us know just what that means. We have an "aha" moment. Something within us falls into place, and how we perceive a sliver of reality is never the same again.

Here in our twenty-first century, we stand at the crossroads of what has been and what is yet to come. The urge to explore horizons is in our DNA. Each quantum leap brings us closer to what may have been our beginning and what awaits us at the end. In all our faith traditions, there is, metaphorically, gold, incense, and myrrh. Some symbols have lasting value; some rituals transcend the passage of time; some perceptions are just for the moment. A multidimensional universe birthed a multifaceted planet that continues to give rise to life forms of unending diversity. Again, and yet again, that which is emerging is endlessly evolving, forging a path through the thick undergrowth of countless civilizations in order to live on.

~ ~ ~

QUANTUM SPARKS / QUANTUM SPIRIT
Personal Reflection on the Reading
What did you find most disturbing, and why?
What did you find most liberating and inspiring, and why?
What points are "keepers" for you?

•

Group Discussion
Gather with others to discuss how you feel about what you read.
Encourage all to share their response to the questions raised above.

•

What will you try to put into practice from what was presented here?

•

How might an understanding of Jesus as one seeking refuge
be a blessing here and now?

Closing Prayer
"Take the Time"

TAKE THE TIME

Take the time to sing a song,
for all those people who don't belong:
the women wasted by defeat,
the men condemned to walk the street,
the down and out we'll never meet.

Take the time to say a prayer
for all those people who face despair:
the starving multitudes who pray
to make it through another day,
who watch their children slip away.

Take the time to hear the plea
of every desperate refugee:
the millions who have had to flee
their lands, their loves, their liberty,
who turn in hope to you and me.

Take the time to take a stand
for peace and justice in every land.
Where power causes deep unrest,
come, take the part of the oppressed,
and then, says God, you will be blessed.

Words and Music: Miriam Therese Winter
© Medical Mission Sisters 1987

CHAPTER THREE

TRANSITION

"When they had done everything the Law required, Joseph, Mary, and their baby, Jesus, returned to Galilee. In their home in Nazareth, the child grew to maturity. He was filled with wisdom, and God's favor was with him." (Luke 2:39-40)

We know very little about Jesus during those years of his maturing, and even less about his siblings. Of this, however, we are certain. Jesus was Mary's firstborn, but he was not her only child.

BACKSTORY

After their return to Nazareth, a cloak of silence settled around the narrative of Jesus. It is not clear who knew of the circumstances of his conception. Certainly the religious authorities did, for Joseph had to negotiate with them to take Mary as his wife and give legitimacy to the child. Technically, Jesus was a *mamzer* – an Israelite whose paternity was unknown, which differs from a "bastard." That secret remained throughout his life, and in general, to this day.

There is very little information to shed light on his childhood. Consequently, it is hard to imagine Jesus growing up among his brothers and his sisters with a mother in charge of her brood. However, those are the facts.

Mary gave birth to four other sons: Joseph, James, Jude, and Simon. All four Gospels mention his brothers and his sisters, but not until much later on. For example, when an itinerant Jesus was out interacting with people, he heard that his mother and brothers were outside and were anxious to speak with him. To this, he replied, "Who is my mother? Who are my brothers?" He pointed to his disciples: "Here is my mother. Here are my brothers. Anyone who does the will of God is my brother and sister and mother." Although he had added a metaphorical twist in that situation, the existence of his siblings was factual. (Matt 13:46-50) Mark's Gospel concurs. In Nazareth, on the Sabbath, those who heard him speak, said: "What is this wisdom that has been granted him, and these miracles that are worked through him? Surely, this is the carpenter, the son of Mary, the brother of James and Joseph and Jude and Simon. His sisters, too, are they not here with us?" (Mk 6: 3-4) All this was in the future, but it was necessary to include this historical evidence here in order to make a point. Jesus had siblings. He grew up among sisters and brothers.

It is likely that Mary was protective of Jesus and that he was close to his mom. It is not hard to imagine that he spent a lot of time with her as she set about her daily chores with a watchful eye on her brood. Surely, he was a help to her, looking after the little ones, bringing in wood for the fire, weeding the garden, gathering olives, and tending to the grapevines: tasks that reflected a love for nature and its solitude.

When Jesus was twelve, scripture records, he and his parents went to Jerusalem to celebrate Passover. When they returned home, they left him behind. Days later, they came back for him. He was in the Temple. They saw him conversing with the elders, who were impressed with his intelligent responses to their questions. Had he been preparing for his bar mitzvah, the coming of age ritual for boys? That certainly seems likely. On their return to Nazareth, the narrative goes silent for a very long time. Sources say that he learned a trade from Joseph, who was a carpenter. He also immersed himself in the scriptures and in his environment, deepening his love for all the transformative moments that nature provides. Scripture sums up this lengthy period during which the boy became a man. "He was filled with wisdom, and God's favor was with him."

ANOTHER PERPECTIVE

From his early teens, through young adulthood and a little beyond, a cloud of unknowing hovers over Mary's son. Was his hidden life productive? What was his daily routine? Was he really a carpenter? Perhaps he was more of a hermit …a mystic… a guru or a savant. During all those years, he may have been an itinerant traveler and visited ancient sites, perhaps retracing his parents' footsteps in search of an elusive past.

There is a whole lot implied in the few words cited above. "God's favor was with him." That is the Bible's summary of all those many years of the boy's maturing. A lifetime of living took place in the spaces between the lines, perhaps concealing a wealth of wisdom relevant to our own lives. We are so accustomed to details – to facts, data, conclusions. There is barely room for Spirit to enlighten, energize, inspire. What some folk call speculation, the deeply intuitive see as another way of knowing, one that does not conform. The passage from Luke provides an opportunity to reflect on a deeper level. When we fast-forward to analyze the public presence of Jesus, we see concrete indications of who the child will become. We may even discover that there are similarities between his story and our own.

We forget more than we remember of our own journey to the present moment. There is so much wisdom in those decisive turning points that resulted in who we are now. Perhaps in looking back we will see that past actions or convictions were decisively prophetic. We may have contributed more to the well-being of others than we realize. For me, what seems extraordinary about the life of Jesus is the very ordinary way God's anointed grew into maturity. I see that as a hopeful sign for all of us here and now.

RESURRECTING THE SPIRIT OF JESUS

As this book is coming to birth, we are in a time of transition. Suddenly the whole world is under siege by something we cannot see. A pandemic force has made relative so many of our absolutes, those "absolutely not in my lifetime" stances protecting the status quo. Silently, stealthily, swiftly, a viral contagion we struggle to control is redefining our lives. Boundaries, borders, barriers are no match for this intruder. As I agonize over the impact of Covid-19 on all that has meaning in our lives, I can also see how an unseen Spirit is making a way where there was no way to facilitate essential change. The goodness and generosity of so many people are the beacons of hope that we desperately need. In this tense time of transition, when we do not know the way ahead into an uncertain future, we who are Christian need to ask, what would Jesus do? What path would his preaching and teaching take to help us get through tomorrow as a planet of prayer-full people? As a nation of diverse cultures and contradictory convictions. As a community. Imagine for a moment Gaia singing in a gazillion dialects: "You'll never walk alone." Then reflect on what it really means when we say, "We are all in this together."

QUANTUM SPARKS / QUANTUM SPIRIT
Personal Reflection on the Reading
What did you find most disturbing, and why?
What did you find most liberating or inspiring, and why?
What points are "keepers" for you?

●

Group Discussion
Gather with others to discuss how you feel about what you read.
Encourage all to share their response to the questions raised above.

●

What will you try to put into practice from what was presented here?

•

How can we resurrect the spirit of Jesus among us?
Like him, how might we be a blessing here and now?

Closing Prayer
"Peace Prayer"

PEACE PRAYER

Peace is the prayer we pray for this new world emerging,
for hastening the day of consciousness converging.
Peace flowing from within will alter the way we live,
repairing what has been whenever we forgive.

Build no restraining wall. Resist the violent voices.
Extend a hand to all. Make conscientious choices.
Those forces that divide, hostility and despair,
will never override the good that's everywhere.

When all the world is one and all the wars are ended,
new empathies begun, old enemies befriended;
when accusations cease, when turbulent thoughts are stilled,
perennial dreams of peace will finally be fulfilled.

Words: Miriam Therese Winter
Hymn Tune: NUN DANKET
© Medical Mission Sisters 2000

CHAPTER FOUR

FILLED WITH THE SPIRIT

"Filled with the Holy Spirit, Jesus left the Jordan. For forty days, the Spirit led him through the wilderness, where he was tempted by the devil. With the power of the Spirit in him, he returned to Galilee; and his reputation spread throughout the countryside." (Lk 4:1-2; 14)

BACKSTORY

The sojourn of Jesus in the desert, supposedly for forty days, is a classic scripture reference within Christian tradition during the forty days of Lent. Churches take elements of his experience as reflected in the biblical text and apply these metaphorically to contemporary times. Spiritually, this can be helpful. Liturgically, the situation applies. Factually, well, let us think about that. Read the complete passage in the Bible. The text itself as it appears within our received tradition is heavily metaphorical. As such, its meaning does not transfer literally to us here and now. To do that would call for a modified storyline, one more closely aligned with us, and more likely the way it was. First, we would need to identify those teachable moments preserved from antiquity before we can determine their application to contemporary times.

To begin with, there was growing dissatisfaction in Galilee with regard to social and civic inequities in the time of Jesus. Women, especially widows, and foreigners, were struggling to survive. The impoverished and those who were on the margins were looking for leadership to support a challenge to the status quo. Many began to pressure Jesus to put into practice the words they had heard him preach.

ANOTHER PERPECTIVE

Jesus withdrew to the desert. Increasing political unrest was a sign of a pending challenge that he did not want to accept but knew he could not decline. At the heart of his dilemma was the person he would become. Many wanted him to go public with his revolutionary wisdom. In his heart, he was a man of peace. His inclination toward justice for the outcast and the poor, however, was pulling him into the limelight. There was pressure to assume a more militant form of leadership. To embrace that role meant going down a path of no return.

He retreated to the desert in order to fast and pray and to call upon the Spirit to help him decide. A lengthy sojourn in desert heat while deprived of food and water can wreak havoc with the mind, even if, now and then, one takes a sip from a desert spring and nibbles on some berries. The delegation pressuring him had promised him power and material comfort. They would protect him and keep him safe with armed guards and weapons. Yet this was not his calling. His mission differed from theirs. The support he received in his moment of desperation arose from deep within him.

> *"You must worship God and serve God only.*
> *God will send angels to guard you,*
> *to hold you in their hands and protect you,*
> *lest you stub your foot against a stone."* (Lk 4:10-11)

Jesus came out of the desert committed to letting the Spirit lead him. Luke introduces the Galilean ministry of Jesus with these words:

"With the power of the Spirit in him, Jesus returned to Galilee. His reputation spread throughout the countryside. He taught in their synagogues, and everyone praised him."

(Lk 4:14)

This is the snapshot of Jesus at the beginning of his public ministry. He was a man driven by the Spirit. In the desert, he was an open conduit for Energy already enveloping him. The invisible forces of nature – the ways of the Spirit, not the armaments of destruction – would be his sole support. When he was at his lowest point, a Blessed Reassurance gave him the necessary courage to take that quantum leap.

RESURRECTING THE SPIRIT OF JESUS

"It is the Spirit that gives life.
The words I have spoken to you are spirit and they are life." (John 6:63)

One cannot help but wonder: just how much did the natural world affect Jesus personally. There are many indications that his spirit was open to elemental forces – wind, rain, the rising sun – yet all the while, one of us. Interwoven with the complexities of his humanity was a force that links once upon a time to an ever after. Invisible elements reverberate in Jesus as word made manifest. Transmitted through the centuries are those transformative moments worth handing on, for they reveal dimensions of our species we cannot afford to lose. In our pragmatic, fast-moving world, qualitative links to the transcendent are often in short supply.

Jesus resonated with a passion that transcends triviality. We need to do the same. That happens when we encourage others to reach beyond self-imposed limitations in order to perceive the blueprint of the Divine within us all. Now, more than ever, we need to trust that the Spirit, present from the beginning, will be with us to the end. How can we put into practice this transformative sliver of hope when we live amid such turbulence? Trust incarnate Wisdom. Be open to that invisible force riding the winds of change. When things appear totally out of control, let go of traditional blueprints. Be open to alternative realities, to the underbelly of society. Look at life from the other side. God can bring good out of evil. Hope will conquer despair. There is a way out of the desert. Just ahead is an oasis brimming over with refreshing springs.

QUANTUM SPARKS / QUANTUM SPIRIT
Personal Reflection on the Reading
What did you find most surprising, and why?
What did you find most liberating or inspiring, and why?
What points are "keepers" for you?

•

Group Discussion
Gather with others to discuss how you feel about what you read.
Encourage all to share their response to the questions raised above.

•

What will you try to put into practice from what was presented here?

•

How might the spirit of Jesus be a tangible blessing here and now?

Closing Prayer
"Spirit of God"

SPIRIT OF GOD

Spirit of God at the dawn of creation,
life-giving, loving, and hovering still,
to You we turn in anticipation:
fill the earth, bring it to birth and blow where you will.
Blow, blow, blow till I be
but breath of the Spirit blowing in me.

Here in the midst of a world so conflicted,
caught between forces for good and for ill,
Spirit of love, move unrestricted:
fill the earth, bring it to birth and blow where you will.
Blow, blow, blow till I be
but breath of the Spirit blowing in me.

God's word abounds. The discerning will hear it,
heart linked to heart, linking blessings until
all people know we're one in the Spirit:
fill the earth, bring it to birth and blow where you will.
Blow, blow, blow till I be
but breath of the Spirit blowing in me.

Spirit of God, stir within Your creation.
Make us aware of the gifts You instill.
Open us to a new revelation:
fulfill the earth, bring it to birth
and blow where You will.
Blow, blow, blow till I be
but breath of the Spirit blowing in me.

Words and Music: Miriam Therese Winter
© Medical Mission Sisters 1965, 2002

CHAPTER FIVE

MAN AMONG WOMEN

"Jesus traveled through towns and villages proclaiming the good news of the reign of God. Twelve disciples went with him. So did certain women cured of debilitating ailments or delivered of evil spirits. Among them was Mary of Magdala, no longer possessed by seven demons; Joanna the wife of Chuza, who was Herod's steward; and several other women who provided for all of them out of their own resources." (Lk 8:1-3)

BACKSTORY

Luke's description of this undertaking is both metaphorical and factual. On the one hand, it evokes an image of a traveling road show in rural America during pioneering days. A troupe would arrive in a town unannounced, set up its tents, mingle for a while, then preach, teach, and entertain. While Jesus and his entourage were intrinsically different, both endeavors had this in common. They offered the locals an opportunity to break from their daily routine.

Inevitably, Jesus would stir things up by addressing social issues and economic concerns. Most certainly, he spent hours, even days, hearing the stories of the oppressed and blessing them in return. He was sensitive to the plight of the many who had fallen on hard times. A charismatic preacher, an empathetic presence, a champion of change: this became his mission. It was a politically dangerous one. He spoke on behalf of the destitute: the sick, the outcast, the recluse, the indigent; penniless widows and orphans; those seeking refuge and all those outside the system who would never belong. That is what the Gospel writer meant by describing the ministry of Jesus as "proclaiming the good news." For this Galilean preacher, the phrase would come to represent his understanding of God.

Good news to the disenfranchised is often a threat to the status quo and core to being prophetic. There is always more to learn about what it means to be inclusive of all who are involved. Consider how Luke describes those who decided to accompany Jesus on his charismatic mission. He mentions "twelve disciples" but says nothing at all about them. We know that they are men, because he goes on to describe the women. Ask the females in your circle how they feel about what he writes. "Women cured of debilitating ailments or delivered of evil spirits ... possessed by seven demons." Despite Luke's disparaging description, we know that a diverse cohort of strong, dedicated women did accompany Jesus. They traveled with him to villages and towns where he proclaimed a new and liberating way of being and belonging. Because the group included women, it is likely there were also children.

What do we know about the women associated with Jesus? Sources identify some of them, but many more were anonymous. The women held the purse strings. That in itself says a lot. They would have seen to the well-being of all those traveling together, providing a perspective on the day's events to the benefit of all. Several have the name of Mary. The woman Luke mentions above, one of the first to follow Jesus, grew up on the banks of the Galilean Sea. She knew how to relate to men who would also become disciples, rugged individuals accustomed to the harsh capriciousness of storms and surf and – God willing – nets filled to the point of breaking. There was Salome, whom scripture describes as the mother of Zebedee's sons. She also lived by the sea, and was among the women keeping vigil in the shadows as Jesus hung dying on the cross.

Mary Magdalene grew close to Jesus and was part of his inner circle. A leader among the women, she was with Jesus from the beginning of his short-lived public life, and she would be with him at the end. Also dear to Jesus were the sisters, Martha and Mary, and their brother Lazarus. Theirs was a house he could call home, a sanctuary for rest, good food, lively conversations, and a chance to be out of the limelight. Here he could experience a bit of normality. Here he could shed for a moment the public persona he had become.

Jesus and his entourage traveled to small villages and to thriving towns, proclaiming the good news he had envisioned as the legacy of the Divine. One Sabbath day he went into the synagogue in Nazareth and read this passage from the scroll before sharing his wisdom with them.

"The Spirit has been given to me,
has anointed me,
sent me to bring good news to the poor,
to proclaim liberty to captives,
and new sight to the blind,
to set the downtrodden free
and proclaim the Divine's year of favor." (Lk 4:16-19)

The reputation of Jesus continued to spread throughout the countryside. There were times when Mary, the mother of Jesus, traveled with her son, or stood in the midst of a crowd that had assembled to hear his teachings. Scripture refers to her as the mother of James the younger, and of Joseph. As was customary, the first child Mary conceived with Joseph received his father's name. After the death of Jesus, younger brother James emerged as a leader in Jerusalem. A staunch group of females had publicly supported Jesus during those final days prior to his crucifixion. The daughters of Jerusalem chronicled in Luke had formed the core of a dedicated community that would continue after he was gone.

It is clear from various sources that Jesus made an impact on women. In one way or another, after an encounter with this Galilean sage, women felt liberated, respected, energized, and very often, healed.

He extended an invitation to them to enter into a new way of being in relationship with life. He also assured them of their value to the Divine Spirit present within all.

ANOTHER PERSPECTIVE

Why do women so seldom speak about women in the life of Jesus? Especially now, when women can. Society in general has made great strides to minimize gender bias, yet Christianity continues to recycle the past to avoid systemic change. Meanwhile, Spirit encourages us to go back to the beginning and learn how to begin again. We need to suspend our penchant for facts. Pay attention to the story. Storytelling is the universal genre of oral tradition. It is how we engage our children; how we transmit quintessential values that we cannot bear to lose. "Once upon a time" does not exist in the imagination only. It is core to the foundation of humanity's storyline. What was the real story of Jesus, who was human just like us, and what might that mean for us? Women know that this is a storyline well worth pursuing in these chaotic times. The precursor of history – herstory – lingers in the shadows of what is now the past. Except in a quantum universe, where we encounter an eternal now.

Jesus transmitted essential values primarily through telling stories. His parables – stories that make a point – often embody the core of his teaching with an element of surprise. For example, the following parable (Mt 25:1-13), tells of ten women assembled to accompany a wedding party to their celebratory banquet. After a lengthy delay, they grew weary and fell asleep. All ten awoke to music in the distance. When they proceeded to trim their lamps, five no longer had oil to burn and five had more than enough. The latter joined the caravan and its festive celebration. The others went off to replenish their supply, no small feat in the middle of the night with all doors shut and barred. Eventually, they arrived at the wedding, lamps burning brightly, but the host would not admit them.

Tradition interprets this story as a warning. Be prepared for the final judgment. Make sure you have enough of that which is essential. Now this is where my perspective differs. Precisely what is essential? Enough oil only for yourself with no concern whatever for the well-being of others? If that is the conclusion here, then we need to ask of the text: whose banquet is this anyway? It does not reflect that heavenly feast over which Jesus metaphorically presides. Jesus would have warmly welcomed those five systemically disadvantaged yet very resourceful women. He would have escorted them to those seats reserved as places of honor. We need that same can-do spirit as we lobby on behalf of the common good. We need to show in concrete ways how sharing benefits all. If we want to reflect the spirit of Jesus, take those relegated to the back of the bus straight up to the top of the line ... in religion and society ... now, here, everywhere.

Jesus spent his life lobbying for the disadvantaged. He would share what he had with those in need and turn no one away. There were many then, and many more now, who will never have enough, no matter how hard they try. Denied a seat at the table, they work diligently just to get by, while others who have far more than needed hold onto what they have. The point of this parable is this: share your surplus with those in need, and more than that, if you are able. The quantum spirit of Jesus will ensure there will be enough for all. Enough love. Enough mercy. An endless supply of compassion. This parable focused on women cries out for a woman's perspective, especially in these challenging times.

There is still a lack of female leadership in so many Christian traditions. Manifold are the reasons this discrepancy lingers on. Of this, I am certain: it is not because of Jesus. We cannot attribute this divisive practice to the one who was at ease among women from the beginning of his life right up until the end. They were vital to his mission. Scripture records that the disciples went out to villages and hamlets, establishing new relationships by breaking bread together. Two by two, they traveled. Bit by bit, they initiated a more inclusive way of being in the world. Table fellowship was core to this new mode of belonging, one not based on religious authenticity or biology, but instead, a welcoming inclusion. We assume that those disciples were male, yet how likely is it that doors would open to admit two men who were strangers? It is even less likely that two strange men would be given a place at the family table, no matter how good the news. Two women, however, have a chance of receiving hospitality, especially if a child is with them. The vibes between women quickly transform the definition of stranger to friend.

One can see how a table fellowship became the defining moment for Jesus and those in relationship with him. Women were the force behind this. Women today are finding myriad ways to do the same. Women of faith are resurrecting the can-do/will-do spirit of that first-century we-too movement. We too must influence those decisions made on behalf of us all. We too have a lot to contribute to the future of our children. We too are women energized by a vision of equality. There will always be room at our table. The oil in our lamp may flicker, especially if we continue to share, but the Source of divine abundance will ensure that its flame will never go out.

RESURRECTING THE SPIRIT OF JESUS

Here we are in 2020. Light years from where Earth's women were, once upon a time. It is, in some sense, a second coming, for women held the leadership roles in prehistoric times. We are perched on the brink of beginning again, daring to envision a more fulfilling future for all humankind. Daring to dream of a kinder world, more sensitive and more inclusive. Certainly, some of us are, and our numbers are increasing.

Ironically, simultaneously, we are on the verge of systemic annihilation, as we continue to ignore the warning signs that are evident all around us. Earthquakes, fires, raging storms, and now, an insidious contagion that is crossing planetary borders, no passport required. Ironically, it took a global pandemic that is invisible, sometimes fatal, and disorienting to all, to give rise to the mantra, circulating ad infinitum on our media outlets: "We are all in this together." Even more ironic: that is precisely what Jesus would have said. Now we need to add the question: "What would Jesus do?" Many are already doing that. The world needs many more. As we move into the unchartered territory of an unknown future, take note of the good that is occurring just about everywhere. Kindness and generosity, acts of selfless service by female and male, young and old, of every race, color, culture, creed, and faith tradition, are bringing us together on behalf of the common good. By embracing the chaos together, we will come through it transformed.

QUANTUM SPARKS / QUANTUM SPIRIT
Personal Reflection on the Reading
What did you find most surprising, and why?
What did you find most liberating or inspiring, and why?
What points are "keepers" for you?

•

Group Discussion
Gather with others to discuss how you feel about what you read.
Encourage all to share their response to the questions raised above.

•

What will you try to put into practice from what was presented here?

•

Name one or more ways you might help to foster systemic equality
for women as well as men.

Closing Prayer
"Coming Around Again"

COMING AROUND AGAIN

Coming around again, it is coming around again.
A song of freedom, it is coming around again.
Look all around you: we are women and we are men.
We are singing a song of freedom,
we are coming around again.

Going and growing strong, it is going and growing strong:
the cause of justice, it is going and growing strong.
We'll build a new world in which everyone will belong.
We're promoting the cause of justice,
it is going and growing strong.

Wiping them all away, we'll be wiping them all away.
The tears of sorrow, we'll we wiping them all away.
On that day coming, we'll be practicing what we pray.
We'll be banishing tears of sorrow,
we'll be wiping them all away.

Women as well as men, we'll see women as well as men.
In all things equal, we'll see women as well as men.
The time is coming, we're not telling you where or when.
We'll see all of our children equal,
we'll see women as well as men.

Coming around again, it is coming around again.
A song of freedom, it is coming around again.
Look all around you: we are women and we are men.
We are singing a song of freedom,
we are coming around, coming around,
coming around again.

Words and Music: Miriam Therese Winter
© Medical Mission Sisters 1987

CHAPTER SIX

MIRACLES

"There was a wedding in Cana in Galilee. Jesus and his mother were there. So were his disciples. Late in the day Mary said to her son, "They have no wine." Then she advised the servants: "Do whatever he tells you." (John 2:1-6)

BACKSTORY

Cana was a town just north of Nazareth, home to Mary's sister. Relatives had gathered there to celebrate a family wedding, and Jesus was among them. His disciples were also present. When the festivities were in full swing, Mary took Jesus aside and told him they had run out of wine. What an embarrassing situation for the family of the bride. She said to him, "Do something!" and he did. He took several of the locals aside and told them what had happened. Off they went to their own wine cellars. In this Galilean region, there were vineyards everywhere. Then Jesus told the servants to empty the stone water jars that stood outside the house. When the villagers returned, he told them to pour the wine into the jars. They did as he had directed, filling them to the brim. The miracle here was this. Avid vintners had taken the wine from their own prized collections. The guests were amazed and delighted. Vintage wine – the best wine – appeared at the end, not at the start, and there was more than enough for all.

～ ～ ～

> "Jesus went over to the other side of the Sea of Galilee. A large crowd followed him. He climbed the hillside and sat down. With him were his disciples." (John 6:1-15)

Here is another miracle story especially relevant now. It appears in all four Gospel accounts and deals with the dilemma of how to feed a multitude that had come to hear Jesus speak. While each of the evangelists differs on details in the story, the main point is the same. A large crowd had assembled on the outskirts of civilization. The long hot day was ending. There was no place for this many people to find enough to eat. Jesus asked Peter if they had brought any food with them. A little boy said he had something: five barley loaves and two small fish. He handed these to Jesus. What happened next is legendary. Jesus blessed the gift as if he were offering a prayer before a meal. Suddenly, scripture records, there was enough food for all. There was even some left over, enough to fill twelve baskets, or so the story goes. A miracle, to be sure. Jesus: man of miracles. It was indeed a miracle. A little boy's generosity may have motivated the crowd to open their purses, dig into their pockets, and empty the baskets tucked under their shawls, revealing enough food for all.

～ ～ ～

> "Jesus withdrew to the region of Tyre. He did not want anyone to know he was there, but he was soon recognized. A Syrophoenician woman found him and knelt down at his feet. 'Have mercy on me and my daughter, for she is possessed by a devil.' Jesus did not say a word. She persisted, until the disciples begged him, 'Give her what she wants, she is shouting at us, she will

never go away.' Jesus turned to the woman. 'Is it fair to take the children's food and throw it to the dogs in the house?' 'Yes,' she replied, 'for the house dogs under the table can eat children's scraps.' Jesus responded: 'You may go home happy. The devil has gone out of your daughter.' On arriving home, she found her daughter in bed and the demon gone." (Mark 7:24-30)

At some point in his public life, Jesus left Galilee and crossed over into Tyre and Sidon in southern Phoenicia (now Lebanon). This was Gentile territory and his reputation had preceded him. He had been preaching and teaching a message of inclusion. Many experienced a change of heart. Word of "miracles" began to spread and did not stop at the border. In spite of his efforts to remain out of sight, a deeply troubled woman discovered where he was staying. Resisting all efforts to restrain her, she gained access to Jesus and began to plead her case. Her daughter was completely out of control. Whether by demonic possession, drugs, or psychiatric disturbance, or simply a young girl coming of age, there was no way to subdue the child. "Tell me what to do," she pleaded. Jesus posed a question. Her answer reassured him. He offered her some sage advice and sent her on her way. We learn that harmony returned to the woman's household. Why? We will never know.

ANOTHER PERSPECTIVE

Miracles are in the eye of the beholder or the heart of the believer, evoking a consequence the recipient can identify and claim. They reveal another perspective in the midst of the mundane. To those who are open to serendipity and surprise, miracles are a daily occurrence, and they are everywhere. We have certain set expectations. Suddenly, the unexpected occurs. Signs of generosity reveal that even those who covet wealth will often share with others. We know this from experience. John recorded the Cana incident in his Gospel decades later, saying:

"This was the first of the signs given by Jesus,
and it was given at Cana in Galilee." (2:11)

If water-into-wine was the first of the signs associated with Jesus, what exactly did it signify? It did seem like a miracle. To go from no wine at all to a generous supply of best-of-the-year is indeed a rare occurrence. Some say it would be easier to turn well water into wine than to expect owners of prize-winning vineyards to part with their vintage supply. Perhaps that was precisely the point that Jesus intended to make.

The same holds for the incident involving the loaves and fishes. Does anyone actually believe that those who had gathered to listen to Jesus would go into an isolated area and sit in the hot Mediterranean sun for hours, without any food or water? Especially water… and surely some fruit or a hunk of bread. They were people who lived in the area, who knew what was available – or not – knew how to equip themselves for whatever they chose to do. We carry snacks in purses or pockets nearly everywhere we go, even with fast food options available along the way. The miracle was this: all, or nearly all, had brought something with them. When they held in their hands what they had planned to eat, the spirit of Jesus inspired them to make sure there was food for all. A little child had initiated a chain reaction. Similar situations exist today. We need many more such miracles in these tumultuous times, and they are beginning to occur.

The case of the Syrophoenician woman is multifaceted and intriguing. Why was Jesus in that region beyond his cultural borders? Was he seeking some understanding of his biological identity? Of his paternity? Was he seeking to discover if there was biracial blood within him? His preaching and teaching, more often than not, were growing more inclusive. He was reaching people at the core, women as well as men. He was welcoming outsiders in. Had he wanted to revisit the cultural context of his early childhood? Search for something familiar? Evoke a memory to support his more inclusive sense of community? He had already preached inclusion well beyond societal limits. The wider world of humanity may have been calling out to him. Was the God of his childhood now – for him – the Divine source within all? That is a possibility. We will never know for sure.

With regard to the many occasions when something out of the ordinary occurred through an intervention of Jesus, let us simply accept the outcome for what it appeared to be in the eye of the beholder. Something out of the ordinary. Something extraordinary. In other words, a miracle. Such miracles do happen. Frequently, we read, in those ancient sources chronicling the life of Jesus. At the same time, we need to remember that what is a miracle for one may not necessarily be for another. Most of us will agree on this: an encounter with the spirit of Jesus can result in something extraordinary. More often not, it offers an opportunity to experience the very best of what ordinary aspires to be.

RESURRECTING THE SPIRIT OF JESUS

We are living in unpredicted and unpredictable times. No one saw this coming – the global pandemic that has pulled the roots of stability and continuity right out from under us. Where does one turn when mired in an unprecedented situation we are powerless to change? Is it enough to do all we can simply to contain the contagion? How do we protect what we absolutely cannot bear to lose? I ask this from a faith perspective. What are the bedrock values that unite us to one another in ways that support our diversity? As institutional religion continues to wane and we question its role in our future, how do we encourage and support the next generation's genuine efforts to help us begin again.

We are living in unprecedented times. We need to discover unprecedented ways to live faith fully in a world that is radically different from whatever has been before. How can we change water into wine, metaphorically? When will we finally hear the cries of those who hunger for food...for justice...for a place at the table where crucial decisions are made? When will we search for ways to ensure there will be enough for everyone? We are part of one another on the level of our DNA. Diversity is our birthright, a privilege, a blessing, and in a quantum universe, we are all one.

The Divine Spirit in Jesus was a source of miracles. The kind of everyday miracles we have come to take for granted. Good news. Good vibes. Good deeds. Miracles resulting from kind words as Divine energy flowed through Jesus to penetrate hardened hearts to prepare them for systemic change. The Divine Spirit is hovering around us and within us all, hoping to catch our attention, for there is work we have to do to make it through a time such as this. We too can affect the outer world in a positive and constructive way through energy from within. The capacity to perceive invisible forces and channel sources of energy is nothing short of a miracle in these tumultuous times. Let us commit to acknowledging at least one miracle every day.

QUANTUM SPARKS / QUANTUM SPIRIT
Personal Reflection on the Reading
What did you find most surprising, and why?
What did you find most liberating or inspiring, and why?
What points are "keepers" for you?

•

Group Discussion
Gather with others to discuss how you feel about what you read.
Encourage all to share their response to the questions raised above.

•

Identify a recent societal or systemic "miracle."

•

What does the word "miracle" mean to you?
Name one or more "miracles" in your own personal life.

Closing Prayer
"We are the Word"

WE ARE THE WORD

Mountains and meadows and free-flowing streams,
gardens and ghettoes and poor people's dreams,
down through the ages the good news is heard:
each of life's pages expresses the Word,
love that engages enfleshes the Word.

  Faith moves mountains, transcending creeds.
  The Word within words is embodied in deeds.
  Fear for the future finds hope in the past,
  for love was the first word, it's surely the last.

Mountains and meadows and free-flowing streams,
gardens and ghettoes and poor people's dreams,
down through the ages the good news is heard:
each of life's pages expresses the Word,
love that engages enfleshes the Word.

  The poor will have privilege, the hungry will eat.
  All of the homeless will dance in the street.
  In God's revelation, real love will release
  the reincarnation of justice and peace.

Mountains and meadows and free-flowing streams,
gardens and ghettoes and poor people's dreams,
down through the ages the good news is heard:
each of life's pages expresses the Word,
love that engages enfleshes the Word.

Words and Music: Miriam Therese Winter
© Medical Mission Sisters 1987

Part Two

TRANSFORMATIVE VISION
• A NEW AGE •

Envision
the fullness of shalom
on a new path
through tradition
that will surely lead us
home.

CHAPTER SEVEN

HEALING SPIRIT

"As Jesus left Jericho with his disciples, a blind beggar
called out to him: 'Jesus, son of David, have pity on me.'
Jesus stopped and said: 'Come here.' He went to Jesus.
'What do you want me to do for you?' 'Master, let
me see again.' Then Jesus replied, 'Go! Your faith has
saved you.' Suddenly, he could see. He decided to follow
Jesus." (Mark 10:46-52)

BACKSTORY

There are many examples in the Gospels depicting Jesus as one who
heals. It was not something he set out to do. It just happened. More
often than not, such healings interrupted other plans. He was on his
way to somewhere or in the midst of something else when suddenly,
an interruption, and then an intervention. He became a source of
healing because people perceived him to be. All four Gospels testify
to his ability to heal people from all segments of society: people of
status, ordinary folk, and the many who continued to struggle simply
to survive. Young and old. Rich and poor. Female and male. Those
who were Jewish and those who were not. He embodied the proverbial
saying: it happened while he was making other plans. The desperate

and the destitute had faith in him because he had faith in Divine Mercy and the power of compassion flowing from an Eternal Source. In the Gospel according to John, the evangelist concludes his testimony with the following summation:

> "There are also many other things that Jesus did; if every one of them were written down, I suppose that the world itself could not contain the books that would be written." (John 21:24-25)

~ ~ ~

A significant healing occurred early on in Capernaum. It happened right after Jesus had testified to the power of the Spirit in the synagogue in Nazareth. Peter asked him to come home with him. His mother-in-law was critically ill. Jesus went to her bedside. What happened next, we do not know. All three Synoptic gospels concur that the fever left her and that she got up and served him. (Lk 4:34-39]

Hearing this, many more people began to seek him out. He helped two men who were blind gain the ability to see. The first time was in Bethsaida. The second in Jericho, where he healed Bartimaeus. The Synoptic Gospels tell of a paralytic brought to Jesus. So many were present to hear Jesus speak that all the doors and windows were inaccessible, so his cohort took him up on the roof. They lowered the pallet into the room and set it down before Jesus. He said to the man, "Stand up! Walk!" Scripture says he did.

The homeland of Jesus was about the size of New Jersey and remained under Roman occupation for his entire life. He developed his public persona through his charismatic preaching and teaching in the area most familiar to him, the northern territory of Galilee. South of that was Samaria. It had a mixed population. Many refused to acknowledge Samaritans as Jews. When Jesus visited for the first time, his reputation had preceded him. Stories had circulated widely of the amazing healing powers of the man from Galilee. Not only bodily healing, but also spiritual cleansing, to the point of restoring a supplicant's dignity. Many knew of this, but not everyone.

While Jesus was in the area, a woman came to a well to draw water. (John 2:1-30) It so happened that Jesus had stopped there to rest. He said to her, "Give me a drink." Amazed, she responded: "How is it that you, a Jew, are asking me for a drink? I am a woman of Samaria." Jesus spoke to her at length, told her about living water, and ended his reflection on the Divine with words meant to reassure her. "God is spirit, and those who worship do so in spirit and in truth." By this, he surely meant according to the Spirit's inclusive invitation, not humanity's penchant to divide and set apart.

One of the Bible's most popular parables is that of the Good Samaritan. Jesus praises him as an example of lovingkindness. Here is the context of that startling assertion.

> "A man lying by the side of the road, stripped, badly beaten, and robbed of his possessions, was on the brink of death. A priest and then a Levite saw him, turned away, and passed him by. Then a Samaritan, filled with compassion, went up to him, tended to his wounds, and brought him to an inn. He told the innkeeper to take care of him and proceeded to cover the costs."
> (Lk 10:30-37)

After telling this story to the audience gathered all around him, Jesus posed this question. "Which of the three was a neighbor to the victim?" Their response: "The one who showed mercy." The closing words of Jesus were, "go, now, and do the same."

There was another episode involving a Samaritan. Jesus was on his way to Jerusalem when ten individuals approached him. All were afflicted with leprosy. They pleaded with him to heal them. (Lk 17:11-19). He told them to go to the priests. Somewhere along the way, they realized they were no longer the same. Somehow, healing happened. The only one who returned to thank Jesus was a Samaritan.

ANOTHER PERSPECTIVE

There were all kinds of healings attributed to Jesus that Tradition considers miraculous, or at the very least, extra-ordinary. Most likely, many of those incidents were the result of compassionate listening, or counseling, or sage advice. To be taken seriously. To be heard. To be respected and treated with dignity. To be appreciated and affirmed. The outcomes of such personal experiences are the stuff that people talk about, and embellish, and exaggerate in the retelling.

Take, for example, blindness – an inability to see. Ordinarily, we think of the physical realm, but the metaphysical and metaphorical are also vital to our ability to envision. "How could I have been so blind?" "Why was I unable to see another way of approaching the issue? Another aspect to reality that might change everything? The other person's perspective, even though we disagree?" The phrases: "I see!" or, "I get it!" are also commonplace.

Jesus healed two men of their blindness – Bartimaeus in Jericho and another man in Bethsaida. After an encounter with Jesus, both exclaimed, "I was blind but now I see." Was this a physical healing? Or could they now live the rest of their lives in an entirely different way because they had seen the light. Had they suddenly understood that their inability to envision a meaningful future prevented their achieving fulfillment? "I see!" In both the physical and metaphysical realms, to be able to make such a declaration can be a miracle. I am able to draw this conclusion because I say it all the time, "I see. I get it. Finally! A miracle! I was blind, but now, praise God, I see!" People of faith in our present age often testify to unexplainable occurrences similar to these. Such phenomena are happening everywhere. "If only we had eyes to see." Seeing is believing. Believing is seeing. I was blind but now I see! I have seen the light!

I resonate with the story of Peter's mother-in-law. Not because I have one, but because I can imagine a different storyline, even as the basic text remains the same as recorded. She was in bed, unable to function. Because she was head of her household, everything had come to a halt. Was it a viral infection? A debilitating migraine? An episode of something similar to the flu? Or had she simply had enough. Her son-in-law had run off to become a disciple of an itinerant teacher. Sometimes her daughter joined him, taking the grandchildren with her, leaving her on her own. Life was not worth living. All she had cherished had changed. Then suddenly, like a slowly dissipating mist revealing bits of sunlight dancing on the crest of the sea, a voice… the voice of Jesus … calling her name … gently, kindly, compassionately, lifting her out of the depths of despair into a new day dawning. She got up and joined her family for a festive meal. That is when she came to know for herself what all the fuss was about. It is conceivable that she also joined the itinerant group of women who were already accompanying Jesus. After all, that is where the action was, and her family was already with him.

What is especially intriguing about Jesus are his encounters with Samaritans. Even though avoidance was mandated, and at best, politically correct, he seems drawn to interact with them, as a moth is attracted to a flame. There was a soft spot within Jesus for those considered "others," meaning, "not our kind". One who has felt deep pain first-hand is often the person who is able to comprehend the pain of the "other." As one who was "outsider" by birth yet raised to feel he really belongs, Jesus could be passionate about inviting the outsider in. Did facilitating healing in another contribute to his own inner healing? Was his concern for female victims of discrimination a way to honor his mother who, among the sacrosanct, would have had a similar status? It certainly seems that way.

In one sense, Jesus went viral in an age before the internet. Using another source of energy, that of the Holy Spirit, he channeled vibes to awaken energies that had the capacity to heal, thereby energizing the recipient in return. This manner of healing from within was common among the ancients and indigenous peoples. It remains a mystery to us.

RESURRECTING THE SPIRIT OF JESUS

I am writing this in the midst of the coronavirus pandemic. It is painfully apparent that here is an unmistakable sign telling us to stop, look, listen.

Catastrophic consequences are barreling down the tracks. We seriously need to reconsider our own routine behaviors, reorder our priorities, and pay attention to planetary issues while we still can. Although the effects of this viral onslaught are truly devastating, signs of a new way of seeing and of being in the world together are appearing all around us. Human beings being human. Feeding the hungry, supporting the elderly, coalescing energies so that those who are in need will know that they are not alone. The selfless generosity of countless individuals and creative group initiatives are resurrecting the spirit of Jesus, blessing everyone.

The mantra of my community is that we be a healing presence at the heart of a wounded world. Anywhere and everywhere. In relationship with any and all. Aware that the power of one plus one will swiftly multiply, I offer this mantra to all: be a healing presence. Quantum energies in and around us provide a blessed assurance that we can transcend self-centeredness in times such as these. May the emerging generation help us to take that quantum leap into a new way of being in the world where all are truly one: a multifaceted tapestry of quantum Energy.

QUANTUM SPARKS / QUANTUM SPIRIT
Personal Reflection on the Reading
What did you find most surprising, and why?
What did you find most liberating or inspiring, and why?
What points are "keepers" for you?

•

Group Discussion
Gather with others to discuss how you feel about what you read.
Encourage all to share their response to the questions raised above.

•

What will you try to put into practice from what was presented here?

•

How might the spirit of Jesus go viral as a blessing here and now?

Closing Prayer
"Heal Our Hearts"

HEAL OUR HEARTS

Broken hearts and broken spirits, lives devoid of all delight
sit around our kitchen table, interrupt our sleep at night.
All the words of love unspoken, all the wounds we have incurred,
all the hurt we have inflicted, wait for Love's redeeming word.
    Heal our hearts, O Wounded Healer.
    Everything we've ever done,
    hold within your Healing Spirit. Heal us all, O Healing One.

When we break the ties that bind us to our family, to a friend,
when we know what was forever will be coming to an end,
when relationships we've severed leave a vacuum wide and deep,
when we're haunted by the broken promises we could not keep:
    Heal our lives, O Wounded Healer.
    Everything we've ever done,
    hold within your Healing Spirit. Heal us all, O Healing One.

Villages and teeming cities suffer from the wounds of war.
When revenge is all that matters, tombstones are for keeping score.
Violence violates our children. Surely, there's a better way.
For the healing of the nations and the children, let us pray:
    Heal our world, O Wounded Healer.
    Everything we've ever done,
    hold within your Healing Spirit. Heal us all, O Healing One.

Pristine waterways polluted, open spaces overrun,
forests felled, their trees uprooted, grasslands burning in the sun.
Daily, species face extinction. As they fall into the void:
one by one, a hope extinguished; one by one, a dream destroyed.
    Heal our planet, Wounded Healer.
    Everything we've ever done,
    hold within your Healing Spirit. Heal us all, O Healing One.

Words: Miriam Therese Winter / Music: Don McKeever
© Medical Mission Sisters 1999

CHAPTER EIGHT

COMPASSIONATE SPIRIT

"Jesus embarked on a tour through all the towns and villages, teaching in their synagogues, proclaiming the good news of the reign of God, and curing all kinds of diseases and sickness. When he saw the crowds, he felt compassion for them, because they were harassed and dejected, like sheep without a shepherd." (Mt 9:35-36)

BACKSTORY

As time went on, the crowds that assembled to listen to Jesus were large, diverse, and eager to hear a word of hope. He felt sorry for them. So many were in need. In village after village and in town after town, his response to individuals was one of genuine concern. Their burdens, while often personal, were also systemic, for social and economic disparity were crippling and widespread. In Matthew's Gospel, we read a second time: "When Jesus went out he saw a great multitude; and he was moved with compassion for them."(Mt 14:14-21) Compassion for all of them, one by one, trapped in a socio/economic reality from which there was no release. The crowds fueled his political fervor, but it was the individual stories that wreaked havoc in his heart. Here are several examples.

Having traveled by boat along the eastern shore of the Sea of Galilee, Jesus disembarked in the territory of the Gerasenes, who were Hellenistic Jews. (Luke 8:26-39) The majority among them were worshippers of Zeus, who sacrificed swine on their altars. Many were skilled in woodcarving and handcrafted jewelry, which meant that their source of revenue depended on visitors stopping by.

As soon as Jesus had disembarked, a victim of demonic possession confronted him. The man, who was naked and wildly incoherent, had been living in the tombs, under guard, restrained by chains and shackles. In agony, he pointed to a herd of swine feeding on the hillside and begged Jesus to let the demons enter them. That is precisely what happened. Jesus commanded the unclean spirit to come out of the man. The herd rushed headlong down the hill, into the lake, and drowned. Their shepherds ran off to spread the news and returned with many others who wanted to see for themselves what had happened. Much to their surprise, there was the once incoherent man, now fully clothed and calmly attentive, sitting at the feet of Jesus. As a result, many were afraid, and they asked Jesus to leave. The man now freed of demonic possession begged Jesus to allow him to go with him. Jesus said, "Return to your own home, and declare how much God has done for you." That is precisely what he did.

Jesus returned to Nazareth, where a large crowd was waiting for him. Jairus, a synagogue official, pleaded with Jesus to come home with him, for his twelve-year-old daughter was dying. He led the way and the crowd went with them. At first, no one noticed the woman who suffered from an incurable hemorrhage. Twelve years of vaginal bleeding that physicians were unable to cure rendered everything she touched unclean. She managed to get close enough to Jesus to touch the fringe of his garment. Instantly, the hemorrhage ceased. Jesus said, "Who touched me?" Peter responded, "It is the crowd pushing up against us." Jesus persisted. "Somebody touched me. I felt power flow out of me." The terrified woman fell at his feet and told him she had touched him, and why. She was desperate, she said, and then cured! Instantly! Jesus responded, "My daughter, your faith has restored you to health. Go in peace." (Luke 8:43-49)

The entourage continued on to the house of Jairus, where people outside were weeping and wailing, for the little girl had died. Jesus went upstairs, into her room, and said, *Talitha kum*! Aramaic for "Little girl, get up!" Scripture says she did. Jesus told her mother that it was okay to give her something to eat, for the child had said she was hungry. He then told all the mourners, "She is not dead. She is only sleeping." The mood of all assembled became one of jubilant celebration.

ANOTHER PERSPECTIVE

Compassion is a feeling of profound empathy, a heartfelt sorrow for another afflicted by misfortune. A sympathetic consciousness of someone else's distress defines Jesus of Nazareth, giving rise to a desire within to alleviate another's pain. One has to wonder how he acquired that ability to empathize with others. Not only to feel how they were feeling, but immediately – instinctively – proceed to do something about it. Was it because, from the beginning, he was mama's boy, whom she was intent on shielding from the cold, hard facts of life? Was his mother Mary the reason he was able to take the cards dealt him and play a winning hand? Were the circumstances that gave life to him the driving force compelling him to welcome the outsider in? Was Mary's own experience of exclusion, which she transformed into a welcoming place for everyone at her table, core to his ministry? Was his innate ability to heal the deeply wounded a skill he had learned at home? It very well may be. Jesus seems systemically prone to feature and favor those considered least, always last, insignificant, burdensome, not worth worrying about.

Let us return to the stories featured in this chapter and consider just what those stories were about. The first focused on a man who was possessed by demons. Jesus encountered him in territory off limits to Jews. In other words, the son of Mary really should not have been there. The afflicted one lived in isolation, under restraint, shunned by everyone, yet he managed to break free in order to throw himself at the mercy of a stranger from Galilee. There is no point in trying to rationalize an occurrence outside the norms of nature. Something amazing happened. Something super-natural. Beyond the ordinary. Extra-ordinary. The storyline handed down to us preserves only the essentials of its beginning and its end. Like our modern day tweets on twitter. It is up to us to fill in the blanks between the written record and those lingering questions left to our own imaginations and personal struggles to survive. The demonic is all around us. Sometimes it is within. It takes a phenomenal effort to break free of the constraints that bind us to our inner demons and to outdated modalities.

The second and third accounts of an old woman and a very young girl weave in and out of each other, suggesting the pairing was intentional. What was the reason for having two separate stories chronicling two different events preserved so that they merge and intertwine? To make a very important point that has relevance to this day.

The story of the woman with a flow of blood long past menopause appears in all three Synoptic Gospels. It interrupts a second narrative about a young girl approaching puberty. Underlying the specifics of these two events is a message that Jesus would publicly proclaim through actions, which often speak louder than words. An unrelenting vaginal hemorrhage excluded the elderly female from social, political, and religious equity. Deemed perpetually unclean, she was dead to society, cast off and set aside. By reaching out to Jesus, by taking hold of his garment, that woman claimed her power and publicly declared her worth. Jesus affirmed her tenacity. Yes, her renewed persona had come directly from him, but it was the result of her own courage and determination. Feminist, womanist, *muherista* – potentially all liberated women – celebrate this pivotal and transformative text.

The girl who was twelve years old was on the verge of becoming a woman. She very likely was experiencing the onset of menstruation, and may have felt overwhelmed by all that this implied, given societal circumstances for females at that time. The affirming presence of Jesus, advocate for equity and equality for victims of discrimination, chronicles a defining moment. A girl's transition from childhood to adulthood is a significant rite of passage. A mother feels a sense of loss as her baby takes a giant step on the path to becoming an adult. One thing here is certain for both. So much of what had been before will never be the same again. Jesus was well aware of the rough path that lay ahead as the female child took her place within a male society. He chose to stand beside her. Eat, drink, and be merry indeed. Celebrate a young girl's coming of age. Drink to female tenacity in a world dominated by men.

There are many stories chronicling the public ministry of Jesus in the sacred texts. These often reveal the compassionate approach of Mary's eldest child. This is such an important emphasis. In a world that is spinning out of control as it tries to sever its links to the past, Jesus offers a vitally needed perspective for today. What is here is not the whole story – no story ever is. It is simply an effort to convey the very best of a life lived in the midst of contemporary challenges. His words remain relevant now.

> "Be compassionate as the Divine is compassionate.
> Do not judge and you will not be judged;
> do not condemn and you will not be condemned; grant
> pardon and you will be pardoned. Give, and there will
> be gifts for you: a full measure, pressed down, shaken
> together, and running over will be poured into your lap;
> because the amount you measure out is the amount you
> will be given back." (Lk 6:36-38)

RESURRECTING THE SPIRIT OF JESUS

During the present chaos, I pause now and then throughout the day and open my heart to the universe. What would Jesus do? The answers are all around me. In the daily paper, on the evening news, cascading across the internet, downloaded into my email account, and periodically, courtesy of Zoom, confronting me face to face. Generosity and loving kindness are rampant everywhere. So is the powerfully transformative force we simply call compassion. Society defines this as a deeply felt emotion triggered by the distress of another and the desire to do something about it. From what we see all around us, compassion is also contagious. It too spreads through personal interaction with another, through countless efforts to help or heal that leap from hand to heart to home in ways that are transformative, lifesaving, and life giving.

While that which we cannot completely control will be with us always, the good that so many choose to do will define us all in the end. Sometimes there is only a fleeting glimpse of hope within the chaotic. Sometimes that is all we need. What follows is the ultimate challenge: to ensure that this lives on and exponentially multiplies. Such a sense of possibility in the midst of what seemed impossible was enough for Jesus, as daily he came face to face with forces determined to divide. It can be a clarion call for us to increase and multiply every act of human kindness in the spirit of one who has shown us how every human face is mirror image of the Divine. In these turbulent and sometimes terrifying times, in the wellsprings of human empathy, let us see the face of God.

QUANTUM SPARKS / QUANTUM SPIRIT
Personal Reflection on the Reading
What did you find most surprising, and why?
What did you find most liberating or inspiring, and why?
What points are "keepers" for you?

●

Group Discussion
Gather with others to discuss how you feel about what you read.
Encourage all to share their response to the questions raised above.

●

What will you try to put into practice from what was presented here?

●

How might the spirit of Jesus go viral as a blessing here and now?

Closing Prayer
"I Am the One"

I AM THE ONE

I am the rays of the rising sun,
snow on the mountains of the moon,
the far-flung canopy of stars,
the shadows of late afternoon.

I am the wisdom of the sage.
I am the refuge of all who weep.
I am the mother of all who live.
I am the promises I keep.

I am the one who sits with sorrow. I am the one who feels your pain.
I am the hope of your tomorrow. When all is lost, I still remain.
I am the one who will remain.

I am the seed that longs to bloom,
the river yearning for the sea,
the heartfelt hope of every womb.
I am the faith you place in me.

I am the silence and the sound,
the gentle rain that breaks the stone.
I am the dream of love unbound.
I am the way that calls you home.

I am the one who sits with sorrow. I am the one who feels your pain.
I am the hope of your tomorrow. When all is lost, I will remain.
I am the one. I still remain.

Words: Miriam Therese Winter & Janis Ian
© Medical Mission Sisters 1987; 2011; and Rude Girl 2011

Chapter Nine

Loving Spirit

"I give to you a new commandment:
love one another; just as I have loved you.
By this love you have for one another,
everyone will know you are my disciples."
(John 13:34-35)

BACKSTORY

The scripture cited above sums up the fundamental ethos of the mission and ministry of Jesus. One might say those words were his marching orders to his loyal and steadfast followers, both women and men. Words such as these have a rippling effect, spreading out and drawing in, over and over again. This was the essence of what he believed and so passionately put into practice. It was what he tried to give to others, what he wanted to endure. It was, in his own words, a new commandment. "Love one another, as I have loved you."

The commandment to love was foundational to his own faith tradition. "You shall love your God with all your heart, with all your soul, with all your strength." (Deut 6:5) "You must love your neighbor as yourself." (Lev 19:18) This emphasis on love was core to a more fully inclusive spirit that emerged within Jesus, a development that went hand in hand with a growing passion for justice. As he went out among people, day after day, and was an advocate for them, it was no longer sufficient for him to obey the laws and do no evil. Those he met hungered for more: a sense of inclusion, respect, belonging, and yes, a place at the table.

One day, a lawyer asked him, "What must I do to merit eternal life?" Jesus responded, "What is written in the Law?" He replied: "You must love the Lord your God with all your heart, with all your soul, with all your strength, and with all your mind, and your neighbor as yourself." Precisely what Jesus had been proclaiming. "Do this," said Jesus, "and that which you seek will be yours." (Luke 10:23-28) What was core to Jewish identity and dear to the heart of Jesus would become the cornerstone for a more fully inclusive vision. In his Gospel, Luke captures the essence of this prophetic message when he chronicles what Jesus said about love to a large and diverse crowd.

"I say this to you who are listening: Love your enemies. Do good to all who hate you, bless those who curse you, and pray for those who treat you badly. If a person slaps you on the cheek, present the other as well. To the one who takes your cloak from you, do not refuse your tunic. Give to everyone who asks. As for the one who robs you, do not ask for your property back. Treat others as you would like to be treated. If you love only those who love you, what thanks can you expect? Even sinners love those who love them. If you do good to those who do good to you, what thanks can you expect? For even sinners do that much. And if you lend to those from whom you hope to receive, what thanks can you expect? Even sinners lend to sinners to get back the same amount. Instead, love your enemies, do good, lend without any hope of return; and you will have a great reward." (Luke 6:27-35)

ANOTHER PERSPECTIVE

One needs to reflect quietly, and deeply, on what Jesus really meant by proclaiming "a new commandment." It sounds just like the foundational mandate within his Jewish tradition. In a certain sense, it is. The quantum leap inherent here lies in an understanding of the extent of its application. It included all people. His new commandment was his tradition's commandment taking a quantum leap to welcome all – unconditionally – in a new and fully inclusive network joined together in love. Its communal roots were anywhere that people come together: the home, at work, the corner shop, the village park, the ship at sea. It was a potential sanctuary for those who live out their lives alone. Criteria for belonging? None relating to religion, race, culture, class, gender, or societal status. The single mandate applicable to all was, "Love one another, as I have loved you."

Most Christians would agree that "love" is core to the fundamental message, and meaning, of Jesus. Ironically, texts in the Synoptic Gospels seldom record Jesus using that word. Yet those with eyes to envision, who are able to hear the unspoken word, can discern the fundamental ethos underlying all of his words and actions. "Love one another, as I have loved you." (John 15:12)

John, the beloved disciple, is an epithet John gave himself when writing about his experiences years after Jesus died. "The disciple whom Jesus loved" is a phrase that appears six times in his Gospel; and nowhere else. That does not mean it is invalid. Nor does it mean it is Gospel truth. Jesus spoke about loving everyone. He certainly loved John. He was the youngest disciple, often with Jesus out in the field and in situations of significance. From what we read in his Gospel, John must have known a whole lot more than he understood at the time. Relevant here is the fact that his Gospel records the depths of the love Jesus had for his disciples and for all those he encountered. Without John's testimony, that knowledge would be lost.

A second consideration is this. If the gist of the message of Jesus was love, who were the loved ones in his life, beyond his family of origin, his relatives, disciples, and friends? A panoramic view of the years following his return from Jerusalem reveals large, empty spaces, and very little information. There was that period of about twenty years, known generally as his "hidden life," that no one has been able to penetrate.

Traditional understanding is that Jesus never married, yet throughout the ages there has been ongoing speculation on what his private life might have been. This much is certain. He was at heart a mystic. Perhaps the wilderness expanses, the raging tantrums of the sea, the energies of the moon and stars helped him to link the present moment, to eternal tranquility. The limited specifics of his graced humanity leave ample room for all to reimagine an alternative storyline. Although Jesus seldom spoke about love, what he did arose from a wellspring of love rooted in equity and full inclusion. A message he would have us take to heart: actions speak louder than words.

RESURRECTING THE SPIRIT OF JESUS

As I pause to write these words about love, myriad examples of love-made-flesh reflect the presence of Word-made-flesh everywhere around me. Many have moved beyond the question: "What would Jesus do?" Instead, out there in the midst of it all, multiple examples of love incarnate reignite a flicker of hope in these traumatic times. Images on the evening news reveal a reality out of control and on the verge of destruction, when an infinitesimal gesture of love suddenly turns the tide. Opposing forces pause for a moment…authority kneels in solidarity with the opposition. A participant in a protest welcomes someone from the other side. What would Jesus do? He would stand up for justice. He would kneel in prayer on behalf of full inclusion. It is not about winning or losing. It is much too late for that. It is all about moving beyond surviving to redefining what it means to thrive. It is about true equality in all aspects of life, about implementing systemic change – and letting the perpetually marginalized determine what needs to be done and why, and how best to go about it. If we do this in the fully inclusive spirit of Jesus, in the end, love wins.

QUANTUM SPARKS / QUANTUM SPIRIT
Personal Reflection on the Reading
What did you find most surprising, and why?
What points are "keepers" for you?

•

Group Discussion
Gather with others to discuss how you feel about what you read.
Encourage all to share their response to the questions raised above.

•

What will you try to put into practice from what was presented here?

•

How might the witness of Jesus regarding love
go viral as a blessing here and now?

Closing Prayer
"Lovesong"""

LOVESONG

Love is patient. Love is kind,
healing the hurt heart, haunting the mind.
Love will go with you, 'til one day you'll find:
love must leave love behind.

Love is a rainbow conceived in a storm.
Love, in the cold war of life, is warm.
Love will be waiting when evening draws on.
Then one day, love may be gone.

Love is a mountain, certain and strong,
sometimes a silence, sometimes a song.
Love will remember the where and the when.
Come, love, come again.

Love will go tenderly, tenderly by,
teasing to laughter, teaching to cry.
Love will watch lovingly, letting you learn:
some loves never return.

Love will flow on into love without end.
Love will continue to break, to bend.
So soon December, remembering when.
Come, love, come again. Come, love, come again.
Come, love, again.

Words and Music: Miriam Therese Winter
© Medical Mission Sisters 1976

CHAPTER TEN

INCLUSIVE SPIRIT

"Love the Lord your God with all your heart, and
with all your soul, and with all your mind. This is the greatest
and first commandment. And a second is like it: 'You shall love
your neighbor as yourself.' On these two commandments hang
all the law and the prophets." (Mt 22:37-40)

BACKSTORY

A sense of celebration was in the air and a crowd was already forming.
The charismatic Jesus of Nazareth was approaching the city gates.
He always came to Jerusalem for the annual Pesach festivities, but
this time, it was different. His reputation had preceded him. Friends,
followers, and others eager to see him for themselves were forming a
procession. He was riding on a donkey, surrounded by a multitude of
people waving branches of palm. It was an occasion for families and
friends to be dancing in the street, a celebrative aspect of the season,
until it became something more. His popularity, the roar of the crowd,
a sense of solidarity among an exuberant and diverse mob was suddenly
cause for alarm. It was also a defining moment. It would mark the
beginning of a week in time that would change the course of history
from that moment on.

Sunday had been a decisive turning point in the life of Jesus, and Thursday would be another. That day, he and his disciples, his family and his closest friends gathered in an upper room to celebrate what would be his final Passover meal. His female followers in Jerusalem took care of all the details, as women ordinarily do: the arrangement of the seating, the settings on the tables, flowers and the overall décor to create a memorable ambiance, ensuring there was enough room and more than enough food for all. They rehearsed the participation of the children on this special night.

It was a beautiful evening. One by one, the ancient rituals related to food and fellowship linked the present to the past. The breaking and sharing of unleavened bread, a sip of wine from the communal cup, the visible bonds of community, forged an irreversible link between now and forever after.

ANOTHER PERSPECTIVE

The culminating supper Jesus celebrated with his inner circle, women together with men, and with his extended family, would be his final meal before he passed over into glory. It was, in the deepest sense, a pledge of continuity between the present and the future: a bridge between here and hereafter; now here yet nowhere in particular; and potentially, anywhere. The focal point was bread.

Symbolically, bread is life sustaining. Metaphorically, it is culturally conditioned and yields to what is the norm in other civilizations. That which is core to a culture has the capacity to transmit an essential value when designated sacramental. A bond that unifies can be a force transcending finite limitations, representing something more. Our present age is preconditioned to comprehend a quantum leap. So many of the ties that bind us or the elements that transform us, now come to us instantaneously, virtually traveling through time and space before arriving here. What an opportunity for transmitting, authentically and cross-culturally, all those bedrock values that we cannot bear to lose. It is within this framework that John preserved the transformative moment felt and shared by all the disciples, ensuring it lived on. He recorded these words of Jesus spoken to his community shortly before he died.

"The Spirit of truth is with you and is in you.
I will not leave you orphans. I will come back to you.
The world will no longer see me; but you will see me,
because I live and you will live.
On that day, you will understand:
I am in the Divine and you are in me and I am in you."
(John 14:16-18, 20)

In that spirit, Jesus took bread, and according to Jewish tradition, he blessed it, broke it, and shared it – with women, children, and men. It is critically important to know where he was looking when he said those memorable words: "Take, eat, this is my body." He was not looking at the bread. He was addressing those assembled.

This community that had already begun to physically and spiritually embody his values – to love one another, do no harm, stand up for justice, embrace the principles of inclusion and peace – this remnant was charged to continue all that would be left unfinished. That commitment continues to summon those who identify with him. We are to transform life on planet Earth on behalf of all humanity, together with all humanity, sensitive to and appreciative of our diversity. We are to be a living – loving – and fully inclusive community in and through the Spirit. Alas, we have a long way to go to fulfill that transformative vision. Let us never forget that Christianity has deep Jewish roots. Let us welcome elements of change that are milestones on the path as we continue to remember the one who prepared the way for us.

RESURRECTING THE SPIRIT OF JESUS

The fully inclusive spirit of Jesus, when it is flourishing among us, will mean something radically different from what we are seeing now. It will not be about Jesus. It will reflect what Jesus was about: sowing seeds so others might envision a multifaceted community loving one another in a variety of ways.

To achieve this requires a quantum leap, which is happening all the time within the unseen reality of our quantum universe. It is nature's way of coming to be, of continually evolving. We need to become more aware of this. We need to link our good intentions to quantum reality, where there is no definitive separation between before and after. Jesus will join in our efforts, for the spirit of Jesus – the energy of Jesus – the divine and holy energy within Jesus is Holy Spirit energy. That same energy is within us. Together we can take quantum leaps on into infinity. Do good here and now, be a blessing here and now, with repercussions ever after.

Whether we realize it or not, the source of nearly all of our interests – domestic, recreational, political – is quantum energy. The secular world is demonstrating the manifold ways energy is connecting us electronically and virtually, more than ever now in a world redefined by an unseen entity that has become pandemic. The humanity of Jesus, overflowing with the Divine Spirit, is a bridge that we can cross together in order to reach an understanding of those on the other side. The emerging generation already knows this from their own experiences. Globally, in so many ways, we are already one.

Let us commit to the fundamental message of Jesus here and now: we are all in this together. May the struggle for justice and peace, for tolerance and lovingkindness, for mercy and compassion, be the tie that binds us together in a global harmony.

Take This Bread

Take this bread, take this wine, as a promise, as a sign.
The life is yours, the love is mine. Let our life and love combine.

♥

Take this heart. It is yours, every struggle it endures,
All the love it's made to hold, all the warmth, all the cold.

♥

Come among us in return. In your presence, may we learn
that you and I and we are one, and a new life has begun.

~~~

QUANTUM SPARKS / QUANTUM SPIRIT
Personal Reflection on the Reading
What did you find most surprising, and why?
What did you find most liberating or inspiring, and why?
What points are "keepers" for you?

●

Group Discussion
Gather with others to discuss how you feel about what you read.
Encourage all to share their response to the questions raised above.

●

What will you try to put into practice from what was presented here?

●

Reflect on some of the ways we are virtually a global community.
How can we take advantage of our innerconnectedness
as we birth the future together?

Closing Prayer
"We Praise You, God"

"I am in the Divine and you are in me and I am in you."

WE PRAISE YOU, GOD

We praise You, God of all the earth,
and all Your ways we bless.
In You all love begins and ends.
Your universal love transcends
our own dividedness.

We call to You with words we clothe
in cultures of our own.
You rise above all cultic claims
to answer to our many names,
a God as yet unknown.

O Wisdom, wait within us,
wake our weary hearts to praise,
empowering the powerless
and strengthening with gentleness,
till all embrace Your ways.

Our many paths all lead to You
in every time and place.
Our hearts rejoice in serving You,
make all we are and all we do
a channel of Your grace.

We turn to You, O Sacred Source
of hope and harmony.
Our work on earth will not be done,
till human hearts all beat as one
in global unity.

Words: Miriam Therese Winter; Music: Frederick Charles Maker, 1887
© Medical Mission Sisters 1991

CHAPTER ELEVEN

FORGIVING SPIRIT

"Forgive them!
They do not know what they are doing."
(Luke 23:34)

BACKSTORY

It was inevitable. Some among the politically powerful had finally seen enough. Jesus was a serious threat to the status quo. His utopian promises were gaining ground. His spiraling influence was alarming. That flagrant entrance into Jerusalem earlier in the week was the turning point. There was more than enough to charge him with crimes against the system. It was time to do something about it. They plotted a permanent solution.

After Jesus had arrived in Jerusalem amid the cheering throngs, he entered the Temple and began to drive out those who handled the customary currency exchanges, even though they were there legitimately to carry out transactions related to ritual sacrifice. Fees that covered the cost of forgiveness granted through sacrificial offerings were the exclusive domain of the priests. This monetary system stood in stark contrast to the understanding of Jesus regarding the forgiveness of sins. The Temple was a house of prayer, he declared, and not a den of thieves.

From there, Jesus went to Bethany to the home of Simon the leper, where many of his local followers would share a meal with him. To the surprise of all assembled, a woman with an alabaster jar filled with costly ointment approached Jesus and poured all of its contents over his head. His disciples were horrified. What a waste, they whispered to themselves, and to one another. They could have given that to the poor. Jesus, however, praised her. She had anointed him for burial, he said. He had a feeling he would not get out of Jerusalem alive.

A series of events recorded in Mark chronicle the steps leading up to the execution of Jesus. Disciple Judas Iscariot had gone surreptitiously to talk to those in charge. He conspired to hand Jesus over to them and negotiated a price. At the Passover meal Thursday evening, there was an undercurrent of foreboding amidst the festivities. Gospels record that Jesus was aware that Judas planned to betray him. He also had an intuitive sense that when the moment had arrived for Peter to choose sides, his demonstrative and unpredictable friend would deny him. After the festivities were over, as the women tended to domestic chores, Jesus and his inner circle went to the Garden of Gethsemane to take a break and reflect. Exhausted, the disciples fell asleep, while Jesus, filled with anxiety, prayed. He pleaded with his Creator, again and yet again, to deliver him from the inevitable. Several times, he called his disciples and asked them to pray with him. They did, for a little while; but they were so exhausted, they fell asleep again. What happened next was a series of events leading up to a horrific conclusion.

A mob armed with swords and clubs approached the Galileans with orders to apprehend Jesus. Judas had said, "The one I kiss. He is the one." He approached the man who was mentor to him. "Rabbi!" said Judas Iscariot, greeting his Master with a kiss that would change the course of history, ending both their lives. Before the night was over, Judas learned in horror that they were going to crucify Jesus. Overwhelmed with remorse, misery, and guilt, he took his thirty pieces of silver – blood money for betrayal – threw it on the sanctuary floor, and went out and hung himself.

Armed guards took Jesus into custody. When a female servant saw Peter in the courtyard, she said, "You were also with Jesus, the man from Nazareth." "I have no idea what you are talking about," he replied, and walked away. When she saw him again, she told some bystanders, "That man is one of them." He denied it a second time. Then those standing by, said to Peter, "Indeed, you are one of them. Even your speech indicates that you are Galilean." With that, Peter began to curse. He swore he did not know Jesus. At that moment, preserved through oral tradition and recorded in all four Gospels with minimal variations, there occurred a defining moment: a cock began to crow. For the third time. Validating the prediction of Jesus to Peter after their final meal together. Peter would deny knowing him. Three times.

Because the chief priests and the entire governing body could not find sufficient evidence to sentence Jesus to death, they handed him over to Pilate. The guards then mocked and tormented Jesus, crassly and relentlessly, until the morning light.

Pilate, the Roman governor, had ultimate authority in this occupied land. As he sat in the chair of judgement that morning, Pilate received a message from his wife. "Have nothing to do with Jesus. I have been upset all day because of a dream I had about him." Faced with the inevitable, Pilot ceremonially washed his hands of all responsibility, and declared, "I am innocent of the blood of this man." He ordered Jesus to be whipped and then sentenced him to crucifixion. They took the condemned man to the hall where the imperial Roman guards had assembled, and before the entire cohort, he was badly beaten, dressed in purple with a crown of thorns, spit upon, ridiculed, mocked, and harassed with shouts of "Hail, king of Jews."

On the way to his crucifixion, the Roman soldiers stopped a man – Simon from Cyrene – and ordered him to carry the cross for Jesus, who was now too weak to do so. When they reached Golgotha, the place of the skull, they nailed Jesus to the cross and cast lots for his clothing. The sign placed above his head, said: "This is Jesus, King of the Jews." Those who were there heard Jesus say, "Father, forgive them; they do not know what they are doing." Passers-by jeered. "He puts his trust in God. Now let God rescue him." About the ninth hour, Jesus said, "My God, my God, why have you deserted me?" A short time later, he called out again, then released his spirit to the cosmic Spirit and a timeless eternity.

Forbidden to come any closer, women from near and far were watching from a distance. Among them were the women of Jerusalem and many from Galilee. Mary Magdalene; Susanna the mother of Zebedee's sons; and Mary and Martha, the sisters of Lazarus, were with Mary, the mother of Jesus. In the evening, a wealthy man named Joseph, a disciple from Arimathaea, went to claim the body. Pilot gave the order to release Jesus to him. He wrapped the body in a new linen shroud and placed it in his own burial tomb recently hewn out of rock. He rolled a large stone across the entrance before going home. The disciples of Jesus, women and men, now had to face the emptiness of a long and agonizing night. They had lost all hope for the future.

ANOTHER PERSPECTIVE

The brutal death of an innocent man. The silencing of a prophetic voice. That in itself is horrendous. The consequences equally so. Centuries of antisemitism, of blame and accusations, of prejudice and persecution, the beastly reality of Auschwitz, shootings within synagogues – the prejudice continues as the spirit of Jesus, who was a Jew, hovers on the sidelines, longing to embrace us all.

It is time we said it plainly. Roman authority sanctioned and carried out the execution. Roman soldiers nailed Jesus of Nazareth to the cross, yet Judaism has paid the price for this atrocity. In some sense, so has Christianity, for Rome continues to stifle the spirit of Jesus even now. There are, however, glimmers of hope. In the Jubilee Year 2000, Pope John Paul II made a pilgrimage to the Holy Land. Before a massive gathering in Jerusalem – the name means "City of Peace" – the pope urged all to "listen respectfully to one another, seek to discern all that is good and holy in each other's teachings, and cooperate in supporting everything that favors mutual understanding and peace." He offered these encouraging words to all:

> "The Jewish, Christian, and Muslim children and young people present here are a sign of hope and an

incentive for us. Each new generation is a divine gift to the world. If we pass on to them all that is noble and good in our traditions, they will make it blossom …. Let us remember this, and let us help to make this happen."

We have taken some giant steps toward a more fully inclusive embrace of all humanity, but there is still a long road ahead.

The issues that Jesus faced, his choice to stand on the side of justice for those always left behind, are manifold in our lifetime. The loss of a source of energy and all the good that one might have accomplished: opportunity to envision, to love and refuse to count the cost, to spend one's life so that others might know the satisfaction of fulfillment. This is true not only of Jesus. Similar things are happening now to charismatic people and ordinary folk, who act courageously on behalf of the disenfranchised.

The horrifying truth is, very good people, many of whom love Jesus, are not doing what Jesus would do. I assume, for many, the dilemma is this: they cannot see that we have made this inclusive prophet of peace and justice into a weapon of war and a credo for exclusion. Love one another, except … we are all God's people, except … There is so much divisiveness within and among Christian denominations and congregations due to various interpretations of authenticity. Add to that a lengthy list of all those civilizations, all those faith traditions, all those cultural realities that do not fit the bill. What would Jesus do? Weep… and then take action.

Take to the streets and to the internet: to the highways and the byways. Partner with churches, synagogues, mosques, meeting houses, nonpartisan collectives, and justice-based assemblies. Actively support "Black Lives Matter" and all seeking full inclusion. If your place of worship excludes any member of God's creation whose heart holds lovingkindness but differs from the norm, take time to reflect together on the phrase: What would Jesus do? That does not necessarily mean the Jesus of our traditions. What would the historical Jesus do? Listen to his spirit.

If one claims to respect, honor, follow, embrace, and put into practice the fully inclusive spirit of Jesus, that Holy Spirit in and through Jesus, in and through all creation, then let us join hands and hearts together and go out and change the world. Be on the side of justice. Stand up or take a knee. March, engage, reach out, unite, repent, energize, and love one another. Respect and help each other, as Jesus tried to do. He gave fully from the limited capacity of his humanity. Jesus can help us now through a resurrected, unrestricted spirit when we try to live our lives in imitation of him.

In the fullness of his quantum spirit, in and through the Holy Spirit, let us link our own inner spirit to an ever-present source of liberating energy uniting us all here and now. No matter on which side we choose to stand, what genetic stream we come from, whatever our personal spirituality or formal faith persuasion, we are all one entity – we are humanity. How can we be people of peace when we are constantly at war over sacramental issues and biological distinctions? We need to deal with that, find ways to unite on essential concerns and walk away from the rest. With all of our genetic diversity, all of our cultural reality, categorically, we are one. The blood of all humanity is red, the same for everyone. No amount of forward thinking, no scientific discovery, no creative, revolutionary commodity will matter if there is no one left on the planet to be a part of it.

Every year Christians commemorate Good Friday. We gather to remember that an innocent man, a compassionate man, was stripped, beaten, bloodied, bound, and brutally crucified. The horrifying reality of crucifixion continues to happen. Far too often, it is because of the color of one's skin. Have you ever stopped to think about the human face of Jesus and what color that may have been? Here is another important point for consideration. Why in the world would we continue to call this Friday "good"? There is nothing good about execution. No justification for taking a life. We need to feel the sting of those final words of Jesus, spoken, in anguish, while dying on a cross. "Abba, forgive them. They do not know what they are doing." We now know what we have to do: eradicate our bigotry, our distorted sense of good and evil, our attitudes toward black and white that lurk around every corner in a gazillion shades of grey, and stop sanctifying execution. Let go of the need to avenge

As we move on into the bright and liberating light of resurrection, may our clarion call from 2020 on be the transformative spirit of Jesus rising from the dead. So too, may we also rise, to whatever is the occasion or the opportunity to do justice, live lovingly, and behave inclusively. Let us do this so our children have faith and so our faith will not lose its children. Forgiveness is core to this death-to-life aspect of Christianity. Echoing through the centuries are those familiar words of Jesus in his personal prayer for all. He told us to pray like this: "Forgive us our debts, as we have forgiven those who are indebted to us." (Mt 6:12) Jesus also said, "If you forgive others their failings, you will be forgiven. If you do not forgive others, you will not." (14-15) Hear the words of Jesus spoken shortly before he died. "Abba! Forgive them! They do not know what they are doing." Let us take those words to heart. Let us try to do as Jesus did. Let us try!

RESURRECTING THE SPIRIT OF JESUS

Forgiveness is core to the reality of the crucifixion of Jesus. It may well be one of the hardest things for humanity to do. We need a whole lot more of that if we hope to come out of our current reality relatively intact. To forgive once is a good thing, but that is only the beginning. "How many times must I forgive someone?" Peter posed that question to Jesus. He thought seven times would be enough. Jesus responded: "Not seven times, but seventy-seven times."(Mt 18:21-22) A metaphor meaning always. Add forgiveness to your daily list of urgent things to do. Help the eternal spirit of Jesus fulfill his earthly mission, a cause worth dying for.

●

We go to war, and we ignore, the homeless poor outside our door.
Forgive us! God of mercy!
For every time we hurt someone; for all that we have left undone.
Forgive us! God of mercy!

~~~

We do not care, we seldom share, are unaware, and so unfair!
Forgive us! God of mercy!
For all the times we failed to pray, encountered need and walked away.
Forgive us! God of mercy!

~~~

We have not tried, are satisfied, while others cried, and many died:
Forgive us! God of mercy!
For times we have withheld our love; for all that we are guilty of:
Forgive us! God of mercy!

~~~

QUANTUM SPARKS / QUANTUM SPIRIT
Personal Reflection on the Reading
What did you find most surprising, and why?
What did you find most disturbing, and why?
What did you find most liberating or inspiring, and why?
What points are "keepers" for you?

•

Group Discussion
Gather with others to discuss how you feel about what you read.
Encourage all to share their response to the questions raised above.

•

What will you try to put into practice from what was presented here?

•

Reflect on some of the ways we are virtually a global community.
How can our interconnectedness be more of a benefit to all?
How can an innerconnectedness benefit a wounded world?

•

Closing Prayer
"O Sacred Source"

O SACRED SOURCE

O Sacred Source, surround us with forces that will heal
the anguish all around us, the misery we feel.
The suffering of Jesus is mirrored in our own,
and when our heartache eases, we know we're not alone.

The wounds we have inflicted through violence and war,
through evil unrestricted, still unaccounted for,
is suffering of Jesus, humanity's disgrace.
The separation ceases. We see him face to face.

The kind word left unspoken, the faithful friend betrayed,
the promises we've broken, the lame excuses made:
the suffering of Jesus, both now as well as then,
each loving act appeases; we reconcile again.

How sacred is this season when dying is transformed.
Through silencing of reason, the stone cold heart is warmed.
The suffering of Jesus, transcending time and place,
is paradigm that frees us, is paradox of grace.

Words: Miriam Therese Winter; © Medical Mission Sisters 2007
Music: PASSION CHORALE (melody, Hans Leo
Hassler, 1601; harmony, J.S. Bach, 1729)

Chapter Twelve

Quantum Spirit

"Do not cling to me!"
(John 20:17)

BACKSTORY

Once the guards had left, and the killing field was deserted, women from the surrounding regions reluctantly returned to their homes. Galilean men had long since departed, fearful for their safety. The women of Jerusalem ended their vigil and took the grieving mother of Jesus and the female disciples from Galilee to safe quarters for the night. It is doubtful anyone slept after that devastating day.

Very early in the morning, before the sun had risen and others had not yet arrived, Mary Magdalene returned to the tomb. The stone securing the crypt was gone. The interior was empty. As if in a trance, she sensed a presence, and assumed it was the caretaker. "My master is not in the tomb," she cried. "Tell me where they have put him." Then out of the depths of the morning mist, she heard him call her name. "Mary!" She knew that this was Jesus. She heard his voice, felt his presence. "Do not cling to me," he said. "Do not hang on to what has been. I am returning to my Source." The mirage ended. He was gone. Suddenly she knew beyond any doubt that he would always be with them, as real as a whisper in the wind or a dewdrop on the grass. The magical moment ended, but the miracle would live on.

There were many similar occurrences during the weeks leading up to Pentecost, but only among the women. The mother of Jesus was one of the first to experience his living presence. For Joanna, it was the same. "He lives," they would say, "he is with us." Their deeply intuitive nature knew this was absolutely so. They felt his spirit within. Believing, for them, was seeing what is not perceptible to the eye. There were encounters everywhere. On the road to Emmaus. At a meal with an absolute stranger during the breaking of bread. The men found much of this hard to believe. They said it was impossible.

Those were difficult days for the Galilean disciples. Life had lost its meaning for many during the period between the crucifixion and the turning point at Pentecost. Some of the men went back to the sea, others returned to the lives they had known before they committed to Jesus. Accounts in the Gospels vary, giving credence to the saying that perspective, good or bad, is in the eye of the beholder.

The celebration of the Feast of Weeks on the 50th day after Passover was an occasion for the scattered remnant of those close to Jesus to reconvene and remember. That included quite a few: the Galilean contingent, the faithful in Jerusalem, and others associated with Jesus in one way or another. They assembled in that same upper room, where the memory of their final meal with Jesus now affected them all. Although the tone was somber, and the threat of being discovered an ever-present danger, there was a palpable undercurrent of positive energy, especially among the women. The female followers of Jesus had continued to keep in touch, surreptitiously, in spite of the risk in claiming allegiance to the executed Nazarene. Intuitively, they knew their time with Jesus was not over. The truth of that feminine instinct would become apparent to everyone.

They were all together in that upper room, longing for some sign of what to do next, craving enlightenment. Their previous lives had ended abruptly at the foot of a cross. Suddenly, something happened. Something they could not explain to each other or to anyone else. The mystical experience was profound. An instant of quantum entanglement, of here and not here, of then and now, forging a single entity in and through the spirit of the loved one who was no longer physically present. They knew there was no going forward without him and there was no going back. This was the decisive turning point. It would live on through the ages. From that moment on, they knew their lives would never be the same. Neither would the world beyond them. Their spirits had merged with the spirit of Jesus. Their transformative experience meant that the history of civilization had also taken a quantum leap.

ANOTHER PERSPECTIVE

Pentecost changed everything. That defining moment in the Upper Room resurrected a firm commitment to continue to the end. Even the men were ecstatic. The urge to share the good news with others drove them out and into the streets, crazy as that might sound when they were enemies under the law. Fortunately, there were other Galileans bustling about everywhere in festive celebration. The cosmopolitan throng included people from far and near, for Jerusalem was a multicultural hub that thrived at times like this. It would be easy for these Galilean strangers to disappear into the crowd. However, this is not what happened. Instead, they called attention to themselves. They greeted strangers, preached good news, ate, drank, were merry as they succumbed to a wave of spirit-driven energy welling up within. This uninhibited euphoria would give them strength to accept in faith whatever lay ahead. In spirit they were one with Jesus, committed to what he dreamed of achieving, acting courageously, perhaps even foolishly, in memory of him.

The disciples of Jesus carried the transformative Pentecostal spirit into their villages and homes. Shabbat meals were jubilant experiences. Jesus was vividly present in spirit. Memory became reality as those assembled broke bread. Phrases such as "he is alive" and "he is still with us" spread through villages and towns. This is the origin of Christian Eucharist, for the earliest experiences of *eucharistia* were in contexts such as these, where women prepared and served a meal, lit and blessed the candles to welcome in the Sabbath. Before long, women also presided over the blessing, breaking, and sharing of bread.

While this fledgling remnant was beginning to emerge more confidently from the shadows, a threatening storm was brewing. Saul of Tarsus – we know him as Paul – was intent on persecuting them. He was responsible for the death of many before he saw the light. He would influence the movement's nascent evolution, sculpt the shape of the Eucharistic rite he had learned of only vicariously, and promote an understanding of Jesus, a man he had never met and one he really did not know.

Scripture recorded the Pentecost moment, not in the Gospels, but in the Acts of the Apostles. This subsequent book is the archival record of an embryonic Church. As such, it reflects a shift in focus from preserving memories of Jesus to information beneficial to an emerging Christianity established in memory of him. Those who had known him personally kept their diaries in their hearts. Others who followed after would look to ecclesiastical records in order to transmit essentials beneficial to the newly emerging Church. The faithful in and around Jerusalem, and the many scattered throughout Galilee and adjacent areas, remained a vital artery for transmitting the living spirit of Jesus long after he was gone.

It is hard to arrive back at the beginning in search of what might have been. Harder still to discern what might be an authentic outcome now. The safest path is through metaphor, where something is and is not, simultaneously, like quantum reality. The words the spirit of Jesus said to Mary at the entrance to an empty tomb are quantum to the core. He told her not to cling to the past, to relinquish what might have been. She had to let go of the one she loved in order to have him always. This is similar to the message given to Moses from the midst of a burning bush when he asked the Divine for a name. "I will be who I will be." The Divine says the same to us. I will be with you as who I will be will I be with you. Whoever you need me to be I will be. In essence: I Am. In Spirit: I am. Whoever you need me to be for you, this is who I Am. This is the gift of the eternal spirit of Jesus to us all. Paradoxically, the legacy of Jesus is to help us give flesh again, and again, to a shifting paradigm. Sometimes, to "lose one's faith" really means that one has finally found it. In the Spirit – the spirit of Jesus – we are anointed and commissioned. We are breath of the Spirit living in and through us all.

RESURRECTING THE SPIRIT OF JESUS

Pentecost

The sound of a whirling wind
fills the house that fear inhabits.
Come, come again, we cry:
break into the cramped rooms
where our hesitant hearts are hiding,
decimate indecisiveness
demolish all self-righteousness
dismantle false securities
rigidities, ideologies
redirect our dependencies
and reconstruct our religious lives,
not from the top down
but from the bottom up,
not from the outside in
but from the inside out,
as it was in the beginning
of the tradition in which we stand.
Can you imagine the mess that would make?
No more than the mess we are making now.
No worse than the mess we are in.
Where Spirit is
there is chaos
and a call for implicate order
made manifest through the relentless demands
of divinity
in and around us.
Spirit of the living God,

You know where to find us
and precisely how to reach us,
engenderimg Pentecost anew
as You blow to bits
again and again
our precious presuppositions
in order to pave a path
here and now
for a radically new creation
in Spirit and in truth.

The above is from an earlier publication, *Paradoxology: Spirituality in a Quantum Universe.* I found myself returning to this Pentecost reflection in these tense and turbulent times. Metaphorically, it suggests a way of moving forward at the deepest level of our blessed and culturally conditioned humanity.

Take to the streets, as Jesus did, and stand up for the disenfranchised, the disinherited, the multitudes searching for hope and crying out for justice. We are all God's people in our graced diversity. Do what Jesus did: feed the hungry; shelter the homeless; help the helpless; support the oppressed; stand up for justice; sit with the lonely; kneel; rise; march! and breathe! Breathe deep until intoxicated with the breath of the Holy Spirit – the spirit of Divine Energy in you, me, everyone, everything that is in the world around us and the cosmic expanse beyond us. Now is our time – the Spirit's time – to take a quantum leap into justice. Liberate Jesus from the doctrinal script that has stifled and defined him. Liberate all those trapped in circumstances imposed upon them. Begin by liberating ourselves from our pseudo-identities, setting free a spirit of love and a firm resolve for justice that will encompass all.

Let 2020 be the beginning of our beginning again. Another decade. Another reality. Another opportunity to make things right for all God's people and for all of God's creation. Indeed these are chaotic times, but please remember this. Chaos is a name for Spirit. Chaos means an opportunity to begin all over again. In the wake of all that is breaking our hearts and testing our resolve for justice is opportunity to change.

Dramatically. Systemically. To take a quantum leap away from archaic Newtonian strategies and take our cue from the universe – a panoply of diversity – where there is plenty of room for all. We are at a point where we have to put our priorities in order, personally and collectively. Our primary genetic category is our humanity. For all our embodied diversity – a multifaceted blessing – categorically, we are one. We emerged from the same primordial slime, a singular stream of evolution, and we are filled to the brim with the cosmic energy of Divine, all-encompassing love. Let us name it, claim it, and share it. Breathe in the breath of the Spirit and exhale justice and love.

QUANTUM SPARKS / QUANTUM SPIRIT
Personal Reflection on the Reading

What did you find most surprising, and why?
What did you find most disturbing, and why?
What did you find most liberating or inspiring, and why?
What points are "keepers" for you?

•

Group Discussion
Gather with others to discuss how to respond to these challenging times.

•

What will you try to put into practice from what was presented here?

•

Reflect on some of the ways we are virtually a global community.
How can we take advantage of our inner-connectedness?

•

Have a potluck meal – those who are able, bring something to share.
Make an effort to invite people from a variety of cultural contexts.
Get to know one another.
Commit to deepening a broader sense of community in your locale.

•

Closing Prayer
"Mystery"

MYSTERY

When I stand on a rolling hill and I look out to the sea,
I can feel the force of freedom finding fellowship with me.
I can hear a call to courage to be all that I might be.
Then I know I have known Mystery. *Refrain*

When I walk through a wooded grove to admire nature's art,
I can feel her weave her wisdom on the webbing of my heart.
I can hear her invitation to be part of all I see.
Then I know I have known Mystery. *Refrain*

As I run through the sunlight and the shadows of the years,
I can feel a strong sensation through the silence of the spheres.
I can hear a call to loving all, to immortality.
Then I know I have known Mystery. *Refrain*

Refrain:
It's the song of the universe, as the aeons fall away.
It's the song that the stars sing and all the planets play.
It's a song to the Power neither you nor I can see.
It's a song to the One who is Mystery.

Words and Music: Miriam Therese Winter
© Medical Mission Sisters 1987

Epilogue
My Journey with Jesus

BACKSTORY

For as long as I can remember, I felt a deep and visceral connection to the world around me. From about the age of three, and throughout my formative years, summer was my time, for me, and nature was my playground. Stars, the moon, the rising sun; the sound of the wind, thunder, rain; a forest of trees, a mountain range; butterflies, stones, a bubbling brook; and always, the song of birds. Summers in the Catskill Mountains were my sanctuary. I was too young to know, that while my spirit merged with the universe, the world beyond was at war. I only knew that the star-studded sky, somehow, was sacred.

I met Jesus when I was seven. According to Roman Catholic Canon Law, I was old enough then to know right from wrong and to receive the Body of Christ, old enough to make a lifelong commitment to the Son of God. In Catechism class, I learned about the Holy Trinity – Father, Son, and Holy Ghost – and other doctrines and dogmas. I learned that I was a sinner and that Jesus had died for my sins, died because of me. There was a happy ending, however, for his death had prepared the way to everlasting life for all faithful believers, and he was now in heaven, waiting up there for me. Did I understand any of that? No … but I loved my new white dress and veil and my little white pocketbook. I also loved the Bible they gave me, with all those pictures of Jesus, especially the ones that showed him in the midst of little children. There was a kindness in his eyes, and I felt a fascination with his flaming Sacred Heart.

On the day of my First Holy Communion, the pipe organ was so loud one could hear it a block away. Clergy clad in dazzling robes processed into the parish Church with incense, candles, and a cascade of holy water. It was an awesome experience of ecclesiastical majesty and otherworldly moments. Jesus was at the center of it all. Despite the pomp and circumstance, I felt very close to Jesus that day, a closeness that has never left me, although how and why have radically changed. That experience was my introduction to the Institutional Church and to the concept of the Trinity – Father, Son, and Holy Ghost. Jesus was the Second Person of that Trinity. He was the Son of God. The only son of God. Even though I had learned in catechism class that we are all children of God, Jesus was God's only son. I did not dare ask how this could be. It was an article of faith, they said, one beyond understanding. Decades later, I would challenge the Church on behalf of both sons and daughters.

ANOTHER PERSPECTIVE

My journey with Jesus covers a span of more than seven decades. I was barely out of high school when I entered the Society of Catholic Medical Missionaries, known around the world as the Medical Mission Sisters. Founded to provide professional medical care to Muslim women in northern India, the Sisters established hospitals, clinics, and nursing schools in Asia, Africa, and other parts of the world for people of all cultures and faith traditions, with no intention of conversion. I felt drawn to that global mission, but at seventeen, had no idea of what I was getting into and no qualifying experience to prepare me for what lay ahead.

I entered the Society in Philadelphia when the founder, Dr. Anna Dengel, was still in residence there. I learned so much from her about people of other cultures, about honoring their traditions, and especially, as a Christian, the importance of establishing a deep connection to the liturgical year. During my probationary period, I strengthened my relationship with the Jesus of Christianity through seasonal rites and rituals. I wholeheartedly embraced a semi-monastic ethos that connected me to what had been the norm worldwide for centuries. Latin was still the language of the Liturgy, the Vatican Council just a rumor, when Medical Mission Sisters, once again, began pioneering.

At our Motherhouse in Philadelphia, we introduced vernacular hymns borrowed from Protestant sources and embraced early on some elements of an emerging Roman Catholic Liturgy. Overseas, several of our missions began to do the same. Because we were often ahead of the curve when it came to significant systemic change and embracing indigenous resources, and because music has always been for us at the core of liturgical celebration, it was clear someone had to study music in order to help us transition from centuries of dependence on ancient sources to whatever lay ahead. Community leadership asked me to consider taking on that role. In my heart, I fiercely resisted. Ultimately, I agreed, and this put me on a path that I could never have envisioned. I know now that it was the Spirit silently summoning me. Those formative years of my postulate, novitiate, and first profession of vows shaped my understanding of our Society's worldwide mission and eventually my call: to be a healing and pioneering presence among everyone, anywhere, accepting and appreciating all.

I received my Bachelor of Music degree from Catholic University in 1964. Emphasis then was on traditional resources: Latin Mass, Divine Office, polyphonic motets. I performed my qualifying recital on the massive pipe organ in the Baltimore Cathedral of Mary Our Queen and never played another note. Six months after receiving my degree, the American Bishops voted in favor of the vernacular in liturgical rites and rituals. The focus would be on parish participation. The intent was to make community prayer comprehensible and more meaningful. That meant finding ways to get people to sing. Together. In church.

This challenge gave rise to another decisive turning point for me. Mass would now be in a language ordinary folk could understand, but I had become proficient in resources that were no longer relevant. While traditional music was fine for choirs, it was not the people's song. People will sing what they are able to sing. Once again, without a plan, or the faintest idea of starting something new, I picked up a guitar, and by the grace of God, have been singing ever since. Not songs of an established ecclesiastical tradition, but songs of faith and hope and love in and through the Holy Spirit focused on the here and now. I sang of healing and beginning again, of Jesus and his concern for the poor, the outcast, and the outsider, and reveled in a new perspective.

"Bit by bit the river grows, till all at once it overflows:
Joy is like the Rain."
The spirit of Jesus, a holy spirit, was at the center of it all. "Blow, blow, blow 'till I be but breath of the Spirit blowing in me."

Many of those songs took off on their own, bringing me into a cosmic relationship with diverse followers of Jesus in an array of Christian congregations and traditions around the world. Bit by bit a singing Spirit was radically transforming me. To share a song with faith-full people of diverse religious traditions meant experiencing a wave of unifying grace revealing we are one.

During those post-Conciliar years, my journey with Jesus as a Medical Mission Sister took an unexpected turn. The teenager who had entered the convent to become a doctor and to serve in the foreign missions realized that systemic exclusion and patriarchal privilege had crippling societal effects in our own nation as well. There was an insurmountable wall separating those with an abundance from those with less than enough. In *Mass for Militants*, I sang:

> Down in the ghetto, the blood flows free.
> There is rebellion in the university.
> Who is the guilty? Is it they, or is it we?
> Lord, have mercy on your people.

Major social justice initiatives, local and global, shaped the core of my inner evolution. Latin American liberation theology, with its preferential option for the poor; feminist/womanist critique and rejection of systemic bias and oppression; the Black Power movement with its resistance to systemic discrimination: these emerging perspectives radically re-oriented my understanding of Jesus. What would Jesus do, here and now? With whom would he align? How would he want us to act?

Years later in Thailand, in a refugee camp for 50,000 emaciated survivors of mass genocide in Kampuchea, I experienced what it felt like to be in the midst of utter devastation, clinging to a shred of hope. During the final days of Advent, in a massive ward filled to overflowing, seasonal metaphors were meaningless and "Bread of Life" in this rice-eating culture was irrelevant. Nevertheless, there was deep meaning here. The child Jesus and these refugees – men, women, and children – shared a life-altering experience. Uprooted, they had left their homes and were running for their lives. Christmas, for me, would never be the same.

I had a similar transformative experience in Ethiopia. In the midst of a devastating famine, in a camp overflowing with starving children, the daily dispensing of life-saving, high-protein biscuits became, for me, a liturgical rite. I entered the space just after dawn, prayed for forgiveness for having contributed to this systemic crisis, distributed what was, in fact, life-saving bread, and blessed all who were huddled in cots everywhere around me. Before long, my heart could no longer distinguish between canonical Eucharist and this ritual reality, for both shared the bread of life.

Beginning in 1974, for three consecutive summers, I joined the faculty of Hope Ecumenical Institute at Tantur in Jerusalem. It was an immersion experience among Christians, Jews, and Muslims, visiting one another's sacred sites, retracing the footsteps of Jesus, getting to know cultural contexts. The past came to life and put familiar biblical texts in perspective, a blessing that accompanies me as I reminisce and write. I sang a song to Jesus – "Loving You" – on the banks of the Sea of Galilee late one afternoon as the sun was setting. It felt like coming full circle in the wake of all that had transpired since the spirit of Jesus gave me "Joy is Like the Rain." I also felt a visceral connection with my own Jewish ancestry welcoming my spirit home.

I cannot recall exactly when I awoke to the realization that I needed to learn more about Jesus from an academic perspective, preferably within a context other than Roman Catholic. McMaster Divinity School in Hamilton, Ontario, was an oasis for me. It prepared me for Princeton Theological Seminary, where an abundance of resources radically reshaped my understanding of Jesus within the context of an emerging Christianity. I met the historical Jesus there, where I eagerly traced the trajectory of the Jesus of Christian traditions on my path to a Ph.D.

During my scholastic immersion, I received an unexpected and unsolicited call to join the core faculty at Hartford Seminary, a historic interfaith and multicultural institution, where I have been for the past 40 years. It is my second home. Both the seminary and my community of Medical Mission Sisters share a pioneering spirit, an openness to and acceptance of all cultural and faith traditions, and a passionate commitment to peace.

At some point along my academic path, a perspective emerging within me finally fell into place. I realized that my sense of solidarity with Gaia – planet Earth – and my penchant for seeing the natural world as the playground of the Divine was in my DNA. I became fascinated with quantum science and the discoveries within astrophysics. I had always understood spirituality to mean experiencing the presence of the Holy Spirit in this world and beyond, invigorating every living thing with potentiality. As I dug deeper into quantum theory, I sensed an integral relationship between science and spirituality.

Quantum spirituality helps me relate to Jesus as a human being filled with the Spirit, one who channeled transformative energy through his humanity. To be like that calls for a quantum leap into the vast unknown, which is the intent of this book.

We need a transformative change in attitude, personally and systemically. Jesus knew that. He lived and preached accordingly. His discourse on Beatitudes as recorded in Matthew (5:1-12) praises the poor in spirit; the gentle; the merciful; the pure in heart; the peacemakers. He stressed that those who mourn will be comforted; those who hunger and thirst for what is right will be satisfied; those persecuted for promoting justice and for supporting the disenfranchised will reap a reward. "Blessed are you when people abuse you and say evil things about you because of me," Jesus said, promising eternal bliss to the persecuted and the prophetic. We need to resurrect the spirit of those Beatitudes and apply them here and now. Over twenty years ago, I named the following eight Be-attitudes as a spiritual practice for myself.

Openness ~ Generosity ~ Kindness ~ Joy ~
Patience ~ Hospitality ~ Serenity ~ Love

Attitudes, or ways, of being, becoming, behaving … ways of being present to others, to life, to God's presence in the world. I have learned that "doing" depends on who we are or want to be, on our being and our becoming. That is the realm where the Spirit hovers, eager to shape and support our emerging this side of eternity.

Through the years, my relationship with Jesus has never wavered, although everything around me and within me continues to shift and change. As the calendar turns yet another page and I reflect on who Jesus has been for me, I feel driven to present yet another perspective on the one at the heart of my call. How ironic it is that Jesus, a universal icon, has failed to unify.

A paradox indeed: that the source of unity for Christians everywhere is the reason for our divisions, even to the point of war. Interpretations of who Jesus was and continues to be are cause for systemic exclusion, and far too often, retribution, even annihilation. We need to change that – now – before the chance to do so is no longer possible and the results irreversible. Only a compassionate underbelly at the core of our shared humanity will enable us to transition successfully to the next phase of our evolving.

I know in the depths of my being that there is no single blueprint that will replicate, *ad infinitum*, who we will become and why. There is instead a shape-shifting sense of being more fully and faithfully human. We do this within a cosmic setting. We are an inseparable part of what Jesuit priest Teilhard de Chardin deemed the Divine Milieu. I sensed this mystery as a child and I continue to evolve within it.

Here is the question I ask myself as I stand on the brink of my own forever after. What is at the core of my faith-filled becoming that is destined to live on? As I look back on the 82 years of my graced existence, I can honestly say that the singular constant in the ever-changing landscape of my life has been the Holy Spirit, all around and deep within me.

The spirit that filled Jesus to the brim, that invisible force inherent in all that was or ever will be, is a quantum energy. Energy that radically transformed Jesus is continually transforming me, merging with my own spirit, integrating my "now" with a "before" and an "ever after." At the heart of this realization is the desire to be open to another perspective in all aspects of life. I have become in many ways a far more inclusive individual through my relationship with the human Jesus. Historically, he pre-dates Christianity, yet I realize that his living spirit continues to live on in me. That creative, quantum spirit is at the core of all I do and all I am becoming. I feel that same sense of oneness with a broad spectrum of individuals who embrace or support the essentials of his legacy, many of whom are Christian. Many more, however, are on other spiritual paths. I rejoice in this realization, and I encourage us all, we human beings, to be the very best manifestation of what a human being can be.

RESURRECTING THE SPIRIT OF JESUS

If Jesus indeed were one of us, then core questions take on a new and challenging urgency. Who would Jesus most likely be and what would Jesus do during a time such as this? What does it mean to embody his Beatitudes here and now? How can we more vigorously promote the vision of a first century villager, locally and globally, in a quantum universe, amid all our diversity? Why is it so urgent that we try to do so? The answer is self-evident: we want the world we live in, and everything we have lived for, to flourish and live on.

For me, this much is certain: Jesus was a human being. The spirit of Jesus is a Divine Spirit – Holy Spirit – a creative, sustaining Energy within and beyond all creation, universally available through multiple channels and paths. That Spirit has been present ever since – and well before – the emergence of *Homo sapiens*, inherent within and all around as humanity diversified. That creating, sustaining Spirit will continue in some form long after we are gone. In the meantime, let us do all that we can with our one precious life to support and sustain this one human family and to cherish the ties that bind us to one another, here and now.

The primary purpose of this book is to help us understand what Jesus was about during the time he lived among us. Consequently, the text is a paradoxical dance between metaphor and fact. Within him was an elemental surge that is at the heart of all that is and all that is becoming. That same Divine Energy is within us all. In so many ways, his life has been and continues to be a blessing. When it comes to Christian traditions, some facts we hold as sacrosanct may not be gospel truth, but neither are they fiction. Jesus was open to the Holy Spirit and his passion was to heal. In the spirit of Jesus, may we also strive to be a healing presence in our multifaceted world.

To the multitudes who are hanging on
by a thin thread of hope
and a slim shred of meaning,
I offer this perspective:
Divine Energy resonating
in and through the spirit of Jesus
is also present in you and me,
in all that ever was and is
and all that ever will be.
We emanate from a sacred Source,
overflow with creative potential,
are remnants of a new way of being
that channels a living Spirit
en route to eternity.

We are called to be a Healing Presence
at the Heart of a Wounded World

Medical Mission Sisters

JOY IS LIKE THE RAIN

I saw raindrops on my window,
Joy is like the rain.
Laughter runs across my pain,
slips away and comes again.
Joy is like the rain.

I saw clouds upon a mountain,
Joy is like a cloud.
Sometimes silver, sometimes gray,
always sun not far away.
Joy is like a cloud.

I saw Christ in wind and thunder,
Joy is tried by storm.
Christ asleep within my boat,
whipped by wind yet still afloat.
Joy is tried by storm.

I saw raindrops on the river,
Joy is like the rain.
Bit by bit the river grows,
till all at once it overflows.
Joy is like the rain.

Words and Music: Miriam Therese Winter
© Medical Mission Sisters 1965

LOVING YOU

Loving you is wind on water, turbulence and storm,
loneliness laced with laughter,
winter into warm.
Loving you is sometimes sunshine even when it's raining.
Loving you means moving on,
part of me remaining.
I'll see you in a million faces before my journey's through,
follow you to a million places for a trace of you.
You're testing me at every turning, where I taste your love anew.
There's nothing lost, it's just the cost of loving you.
Nothing lost, it's the cost of loving you.

Loving you means no returning, always letting go.
Starting over, ever learning,
how well I know.
The One I love is all around me in all the love I'm feeling.
God above, let this love
be your own love's revealing.
I hear you reaching out to me in every anguished cry,
tempting me to stop awhile and watch the seasons by.
As I go, I'll go on living, even as I die.
There's nothing lost, it's just the cost of loving you.
Nothing lost, it's the cost of loving you.
Nothing lost, just the cost of loving you.

Words and Music: Miriam Therese Winter
© Medical Mission Sisters 1976

WE ARE ONE

I am in you are in me, we are one.
What was is over, yet something surreal has begun.
Starlight and shadow and warmth of the sun:
being is what we become when doing is done.

I am in you are in me, we are one,
rooted in that which sustained our life on the run.
Memories and meaning and dreams we have spun
spill over into the hearts of everyone.

I am in you are in me, we are one.
When crossing over, we travel together as one.
Song of the sparrow and dance of the drum:
pulse of a planet at play is what we become.

I am in you are in me, we are one.
Wonderful has been the journey. Regrets? There are none.
Now and forever: love everyone.
Love – real love – remains when our days are done.
Love everlasting remains when our days are done.
Being is what we become when doing is done.

Words and Music: Miriam Therese Winter
© Medical Mission Sisters 2014

HOW BEAUTIFUL

How beautiful, our spacious skies, our amber waves of grain,
our purple mountains as they rise above the fruitful plain.
America! America! God's gracious gifts abound,
and more and more we're grateful for life's bounty all around.

Indigenous and immigrant, our daughters and our sons:
O may we never rest content, 'til all are truly one.
America! America! God grant that we may be
a sisterhood and brotherhood from sea to shining sea.

How beautiful, sincere lament, the wisdom born of tears,
the courage called for to repent the bloodshed through the years.
America! America! God grant that we may be
a nation blessed, with none oppressed, true land of liberty.

How beautiful, two continents, and islands in the sea
that dream of peace, non-violence, all people living free.
Americas! Americas! God grant that we may be
a hemisphere where people here all live in harmony.

Miriam Therese Winter
© Medical Mission Sisters 1993

This text was adapted from "America the Beautiful" by Katherine Lee Bates (1893)
on the occasion of the hymn's 100th anniversary and subsequently published
in *The New Century Hymnal* of the United Church of Christ.
Permission granted to sing these words to the traditional melody,
MATERNA, by Samuel A. Ward, 1882.

Selected Bibliography

• JESUS •

Borg, Marcus J. *Meeting Jesus Again for the First Time. The Historical Jesus and the Heart of Contemporary Faith.* HarperSanFrancisco, 1995.

Borg, Marcus and N.T. Wright. *The Meaning of Jesus: Two Visions."* HarperSanFranciso, 1999.

Chilton, Bruce. *Rabbi Jesus. An Intimate Biography. The Jewish Life and Teachings that Inspired Christianity.* Doubleday, 2000.

Crossan, John Dominic. *Jesus. A Revolutionary Biography. Harper San Francisco, 1989.*

Cullman, Oscar. *Early Christian Worship.* SCM Press Limited,1953.

Cullman, Oscar and F. J. Leenhardt. *Essays on the Lord's Supper.* John Knox Press, 1958.

Fiorenza, Elisabeth Schüssler. *Jesus. Miriam's Child. Sophia's Prophet. Critical Issues in Feminist Christology.* Continuum, 1995.

Funk, Robert W., Roy Hoover, and the Jesus Seminar. *The Five Gospels. What Did Jesus Really Say? The Search for the Authentic Words of Jesus.* HarperSanFrancisco, 1993.

Jeremias, Joachim. *The Eucharistic Words of Jesus.* SCM Press Ltd, 1966.

Miller, Ron. *The Gospel of Thomas. A Guidebook for Spiritual Practice.* Skylight Paths, 2004.

Nolan, Albert. *Jesus Before Christianity.* Orbis 1978.

Pitre, Brant. *Jesus and the Jewish Roots of the Eucharist. Unlocking the Secrets of the Last Supper.* Doubleday, 2011.

Robinson, James M. *The Gospel of Jesus. A Historical Search for the Original Good News.* HarperSanFrancisco, 2005.

Rubenstein, Richard E. *When Jesus Became God. The Struggle to Define Christianity during the Last Days of Rome.* Harcourt, Inc., 1999.

Schaberg, Jane. *The Illegitimacy of Jesus. A Feminist Theological Interpretation of the Infancy Narratives.* Crossroad, 1990.

Spong, John Shelby. *Born of a Woman. A Bishop Rethinks the Birth of Jesus.* HarperSanFrancisco, 1992.

Thurman, Howard. *Jesus and the Disinherited.* Beacon Press, 1976.

Wills, Garry. *What Jesus Meant.* Viking, 2006.

Yoder, John Howard. *The Politics of Jesus.* Eerdmans, 1972.

• QUANTUM REALITY and SPIRITUALITY •

Bohm, David. *Wholeness and the Implicate Order.* Routledge, 1980.

Calleman, Ph.D., Carl Johan. *The Nine Waves of Creation. Quantum Physics, Holographic Evolution, and the Destiny of Humanity.* Bear & Company, 2016.

Capra, Fritjof. *The Tao of Physics. An Exploration of the Parallels Between Modern Physics and Eastern Mysticism.* Shambhala, 2000.

Chopra, Deepak. *Ageless Body, Timeless Mind. The Quantum Alternative to Growing Old.* Harmony Books, 1993.

Chopra, Deepak. *Quantum Healing, Exploring the Frontiers of Mind/Body Medicine.* Bantam, 1989.

Currivan, Jude. *The 8th Chakra. What It Is and How It Can Transform Your Life.* Hay House, Inc., 2006.

Dalai Lama. *The Universe in a Single Atom. The Convergence of Science and Spirituality.* Morgan Road Books, 2005.

Greene, Brian. *Until the End of Time. Mind, Matter, and Our Search for Meaning in an Evolving Universe.* Alfred A. Knopf, *2020.*

Greene, Brian. *The Elegant Universe. Superstrings, Hidden Dimensions, and the Quest for the Ultimate Theory.* Vintage Books, 2000.

Herbert, Nick. *Quantum Reality. Beyond the New Physics. An Excursion into Metaphysics and the Meaning of Reality.* Anchor Books, 1985.

Keepin, William. *Belonging to God. Spirituality, Science, and a Universal Path of Divine Love.* Skylight Paths, 2016.

Levy, Paul. *The Quantum Revelation. A Radical Synthesis of Science and Spirituality.* New York: Select Books, 2018.

Newburg, Andrew et al. *Why God Won't Go Away. Brain Science and the Biology of Belief.* Ballantine Publishing Group, 2001.

O'Murchu, Diarmuid. *Quantum Theology. Spiritual Implications of the New Physics.* Crossroad, 1997.

Phillips, Jan. *Divining the Body. Reclaim the Holiness of Your Physical Self.* Woodstock, VT: Skylight Paths, 2005.

Phipps, Carter. *Evolutionaries. Unlocking the Spiritual and Cultural Potential of Science's Greatest Idea.* Harper, 2012.

Primack, Joel R. and Nancy Abrams. *The View from the Center of the Universe. Discovering Our Extraordinary Place in the Cosmos.* Riverhead Books, 2006.

Ravindra, Ravi. *The Pilgrim Soul. A Path to the Sacred. Transcending World Religions.* Quest Books, 2003, 2014.

Wolf, Fred Alan. *The Spiritual Universe. One Physicist's Vision of Spirit, Soul, Matter, and Self.* Moment Point Press, 1999.

Wolf, Fred Alan. *Taking the Quantum Leap. The New Physics for Non-Scientists.* Harper & Row, 1989.

Zohar, Danah. *The Quantum Self. Human Nature and Consciousness Defined by the New Physics.* Quill/William Morrow, 1990.

Books by Miriam Therese Winter

If You Love. The Story of Anna Dengel.
AuthorHouse, 2016.

Paradoxology. Spirituality in a Quantum Universe. Orbis, 2009.

eucharist with a Small "e." Orbis, 2007.

Out of the Depths. The Story of Ludmila Javarova.
Ordained Roman Catholic Priest. Crossroad, 2002.

The Singer and the Song.
An Autobiography of the Spirit. Orbis, 1999.

The Chronicles of Noah and Her Sisters.
Genesis and Exodus According to Women.
Wipf and Stock, 1995; 2008.

The Gospel According to Mary. A New Testament for Women
Orbis, 1993; 2008.

Songlines.
Hymns, Songs, Rounds, & Refrains for Prayer & Praise.
Crosssroad, 1996.

Defecting in Place:
Women Claiming Responsibility for Their Own Spiritual Lives.
Crossroad, 1994.

WomanWitness. A Feminist Lectionary and Psalter.
Women of the Hebrew Scriptures: Part Two.
Crossroad, 1992.

WomanWisdom. A Feminist Lectionary and Psalter.
Women of the Hebrew Scriptures: Part One.
Crossroad, 1991.

WomanWord: Women of the New Testament.
A Feminist Lectionary and Psalter.
Crossroad, 1990.

WomanPrayer, WomanSong: Resources for Ritual.
Crossroad, 1990.

Why Sing? Toward a Theology of Catholic Church Music.
The Pastoral Press, 1984.

An Anthology of Scripture Songs
Medical Mission Sisters, 1982.

God-with-Us: Resources for Prayer and Praise.
Abingdon, 1979.

Preparing the Way of the Lord. Abingdon, 1978.

RECORDINGS
SONGS AND HYMNS BY
MIRIAM THERESE WINTER

Produced by Dan Paulus / St. Bernadette Institute of Sacred Art
in Albuquerqe & Medical Mission Sisters

Sacred Folk Songs: A Celebration of All Creation
By Performing Artists from Many Traditions
Loving You
Volume One

•

Breath of the Spirit
Volume Two

•

A New Day Dawns
Volume Three

•

Mack Bailey Sings the Songs of Miriam Therese Winter

~~~

Produced by the Medical Mission Sisters
Keepsake
Hymns Re-Imagined
SpiritSong
EarthSong
WomanSong

•

Songs of Promise
Mass for Militants
Mass of a Pilgrim People
[Recorded live at Carnegie Hall]

•

Remember Me
Sandstone
In Love
Seasons
Knock, Knock
I Know the Secret
Joy is Like the Rain

•

For more information:
http://www.medicalmissionsisters.org
215-742-6100

If we believe that we are

not just connected but
that we essentially belong to one another
we will live out of that belief and do what it takes
to nurture, support and further create
the ONENESS we desire.

Medical Mission Sisters and Associates are called to be healers, bridgers of divisions in the different realities
and aspects of life in Africa, Asia, East Asia, Europe, Latin America and North America.

Printed in the United States
By Bookmasters